# THE ULTIMATE GUIDE TO FRIENDSHIP WITH GOD

A STEP-BY-STEP MODEL FOR AN INTIMATE RELATIONSHIP WITH GOD: LEARN TO HEAR HIS VOICE, OVERCOME STRUGGLES, UNDERSTAND YOUR WORTH, & KNOW YOUR PURPOSE!

**Barbara Shirkey**
**Arm In Arm Publishing LLC**

**The Ultimate Guide to Friendship With God**

**ISBN: 978-1-963697-03-2**

**© Copyright 2024 by Arm In Arm Publishing LLC**

**Published by Arm In Arm Publishing LLC.**

Printed in the United States of America.

For more information email
Barbara@ArmInArmPublishing.com

Dear Reader,

Thank you for choosing "The Ultimate Guide to Friendship with God." Your commitment to deepening your relationship with God is truly inspiring, and I am immensely grateful for your support.

To express my appreciation, I am thrilled to offer you a special gift—free flashcards of attributes of God. These ten flashcards are designed to help you expand your worship vocabulary and deepen your understanding of who God is and how great He is.

Each flashcard is a practical tool that highlights a different attribute of God, combining truths, decrees, and scripture. Incorporating these into your daily routine can enrich your prayer life, enhance your worship, and draw you closer to God. They are a tangible reminder of God's infinite qualities and intimate involvement in your life.

Once again, thank you for embarking on this journey with me. Your dedication to your relationship with God will shape your future and empower others to be grounded in faith and friendship with God.

With my deepest appreciation and gratitude,

Barbara Shirkey

Scan the QR code for your FREE flashcards:

# Table of Contents

# JOURNAL ENTRY:

## 2019 Missing Mail

*When I moved, I signed up for notifications from the post office. They'd send me pictures every day of all my mail coming in. I saw on Saturday that I had some Christmas cards come in from friends and some gift cards I had ordered to give as gifts. I went to grab my mail Sunday after church, but my mailbox was hanging wide open, and all of my mail was gone. It took me two days to check with the post office and my carrier to see if they were holding it for some reason. But they said no. It was all stolen! I was so upset! I reminded God how much I was struggling financially and needed those gift cards... I couldn't afford to buy them again... not to mention the Christmas cards from friends... they'd never even know I didn't get their cards... plus there might have been money in some of them. I was desperate. So, I immediately started praying for the person to be saved and overwhelmed with repentance so that they'd bring everything back!*

*The next day, in my quiet time, I talked to the Lord about it again, saying that I really needed them to bring everything back.*

*And the Lord said, "You're looking at this all wrong."*

*So, I asked Him what He meant.*

*He said, "What you're praying for is right (for them to be saved and repent), but your motives and your emphasis (so that they will bring everything back) are all wrong." Then he added, "What if I allowed all of this because I needed you to pray for them to be saved, and I knew you would? What if you're the only person I have in their entire life who's actually praying for them to know Me?"*

*At this, I was gutted! I immediately asked God to forgive me, declared my trust in Him for my finances, and genuinely, wholeheartedly began praying for them to truly become aware of God's love for them and come into a relationship with Him personally.*

# INTRODUCTION

Your relationship with God is the most essential part of being a Christian, and it's the most crucial relationship in your life! When a relationship is new, it can sometimes be awkward—this is NORMAL! Recognizing His voice and knowing His character takes time, just like any human relationship. Everyone starts from a different point: some don't know anything about God, while others have heard good or bad things about Him. It can be challenging to start a relationship with God if you've listened to things that are not true, leading to subconscious misconceptions. However, it doesn't matter where you start because when you spend enough time getting to know Him, you'll see that He is always good, and you can always trust Him.

Most of this book is filled with ideas on how to start getting to know Him. This is NOT a list of "dos and don'ts"; it is a collection of insights, encounters, and encouragements taken from the Bible and my own life. It includes many pages from my private journals of time spent with God and my conversations with Him. This book can be used to foster and champion your relationship with God or even help guide someone you know and love to a deeper relationship with Him.

I must warn you that my "stuff" is not always pretty—you'll see places where I've blown it and where I've succeeded. You'll see the things God shared with me and taught me, as well as times He loved on me and times He corrected me. I hope you'll see how eager He is to have an intimate relationship with you.

# My Inspiration for This Book

When I talk about having intimacy or a relationship with God, people nod as if they understand; however, when I say things like "God told me..." or "God said..." they seem shocked. Once, when I shared my conversation with God about moving to Texas, an older man found it peculiar and intriguing because he'd never heard anyone talk about conversing with God in that way. It was foreign to him that someone could have a natural back-and-forth conversation with God. I have encountered this reaction often, which inspired me to write this book. I am not claiming to be an expert or a professional; I'm simply a girl in love with God, and I want everyone to know how amazing He is. I hope to bring a deeper, genuine understanding and expectation of that level of intimacy with God. He sincerely desires to have that with each one of us. We know this from many scriptures in the Bible, such as Ephesians 1:17: "[For I always pray to] the God of our Lord Jesus Christ, the Father of glory, that He may grant you a spirit of wisdom and revelation [of insight into mysteries and secrets] in the [deep and intimate] knowledge of Him" (*Amplified Bible*, 1987).

A few years ago, I interned as a high-level volunteer at a megachurch in Dallas and was part of their global prophetic team. They held huge conferences with worship leaders and pastors from around the world. We had a special outdoor tent for the prophetic team with ongoing worship, prayer, and prophecy so that anyone could come in anytime during the conference for prayer and a prophetic word. I loved serving in that capacity. However, I was shocked at the number one prayer request from these pastors and worship leaders: "I need to know how to hear God's voice," "How do you know it's God talking?" or "I don't seem to be able to hear God speak." I was deeply moved because I felt the Lord's pain in wanting His sheep to recognize His voice confidently.

The Lord asked me to write this book to help anyone struggling with uncertainty about hearing Him speak to them personally. Let me reiterate that I'm not writing this book because I have all the answers or have achieved complete understanding. I am compelled to share at least what I've learned to date. Yes, there are still times of strain and struggle in my confidence that I'm hearing God. I can tell you that I have grown in my ability to hear Him and know that I am hearing Him. I win more battles than I lose nowadays, and I can see the vast difference in my own life in getting to know God. Like you, I am on this journey of relationship discovery with Him. Through my transparency, I hope you will also see God's heart for you and feel inspired and motivated to continue your journey.

# The Foundation of Friendship With God

The relational nature of the Trinity isn't merely a characteristic of God; it is Who He is. From eternity, the Father, Son, and Holy Spirit have been in a relationship of mutual love and respect. It's a living model of how relationships should be. What's incredible is that God invites us into that divine relationship. Have you ever considered that the God Who spoke stars into space and molded mountains also desires a personal, intimate relationship with you? It's a staggering thought, isn't it? That the Creator of the universe isn't just looking for obedience or worship but for a deep, personal connection with you. This foundational truth about God's nature lays the groundwork for understanding how truly knowing God personally is possible, and He desires and is pursuing us for it.

Throughout this book, you'll see many intimate excerpts—my personal "JOURNAL ENTRIES." Each one will give you insight into ways God has talked with me, and hopefully, you will be inspired as to how He might talk with you.

These excerpts are just glimpses into my ongoing dialogue with God. This dialogue has taught me, molded me, and, above all, shown me the incredible depths of God's love, thoughtfulness, and attention to detail in my life. Sharing these personal moments is meant to encourage you to start or continue your own conversations with God, documenting them in a way that becomes a spiritual legacy—a testament to God's presence and goodness in your life.

# My Leap of Faith

One of my most exhilarating, freeing moments was taking that leap of faith—that the God of the universe, who created all things and sustains them with His word, wants a deep personal relationship with me... He actually wants to talk to ME! For some people, that belief comes easily. That was not the case with me. I remember the constant confusion and mental torment... "Was that God saying He loved me, or was I just telling myself what I wanted to hear?"

There came a definitive moment on one such occasion: I asked God how He felt about me and heard, "I love you!" Immediately, the tormenting started... "God is not talking to you; that's just wishful thinking... you wish He would say that... you're just making it up... etc., etc., etc." At that moment, I can still clearly remember making a choice and declaring to myself, God, and even the devil, "God, Your word says You love me, so I believe this is You saying it right now to me!"

That moment changed me forever! It was the first of many "leaps of faith" I would take to hear and know God and His voice. I say "leaps of faith" because that's exactly how it felt... I had to choose to believe and then leap—based on what God says is true in the Bible! After I made the declaration out loud, I began to thank God for saying it, for loving me, and for letting me hear Him. On and on I went to solidify this new truth in my mind and emotions by an act of my will.

# *JOURNAL ENTRY:*

## *2018 My Prince*

*I was Reading Psalm 118 this morning and came across verse 9. Laughing out loud, I said to the Lord, "I don't trust in any princes, but if You want to give me a prince, Lord..." Then I laid my head back and asked, "Lord, what is a 'prince' to you?"*

*And immediately He said, "One who will treat you like My princess."*

*ME: choked up, moved, loved, grateful, and just about every emotion that goes along with these! HE IS SO GOOD!!!*

# *JOURNAL ENTRY:*

## *2023 Rev. 4:1-11*

*As I read and responded to verse 11 ("You are worthy, O Lord our God, to receive glory, honor, and power"), I imagined the Lord receiving the glory and honor I give Him; however, when I got to the "power" part, I was puzzled...*

*ME: "Lord, how can You receive power if You are ALL-POWERFUL? You have all power at all times to accomplish all of Your will and plans, and You are self-existent, self-containing, self-sustaining, and require nothing outside of Yourself to exist, so how is it that You 'receive' power?"*

*THE LORD: I can receive power that's been given to Me.*

*ME: Lord, how can I possibly give You power?*

*THE LORD: When you invite Me in and make room for Me in every area of your life, you are giving Me the power to transform you... as you relinquish control to Me and trust Me with each area in your life, you give Me the power to help you, heal you, provide for you, give you wisdom, and basically intervene on your behalf however I see fit.*

*ME: LORD COME! I TRUST YOU! I NEED YOU! I GIVE YOU THE POWER IN MY LIFE!*

# SECTION ONE:

# A Sturdy Foundation

# CHAPTER 1:

# ARE YOU A NEW

# CHRISTIAN?

If you are a new Christian, congratulations on making the most crucial decision of your life—making Jesus your Lord and Savior! The Bible says you are a child of God by receiving Jesus Christ into your heart by faith (faith = really believing). So, now that you are a Christian (choosing to live your life in a relationship with and modeled after Christ), what do you do? How does this work? What is expected of you?

## What Just Happened?

Let me first explain, as simply as I can, what happens to you when you become a Christian and the exciting news of what this means for you. Let's look at a few Bible verses about what happened when you became a Christian (*New Living Translation*, 2015, Eph 2:1-5, 8-10):

> 1). Once you were dead because of your disobedience and your many sins.

> 2). You used to live in sin, just like the rest of the world, obeying the devil—the commander of the powers in the unseen world. He is the spirit at work in the hearts of those who refuse to obey God.

3). All of us used to live that way, following the passionate desires and inclinations of our sinful nature. By our very nature, we were subject to God's anger, just like everyone else.

4). But God is so rich in mercy, and he loved us so much,

5). that even though we were dead because of our sins, he gave us life when he raised Christ from the dead. (It is only by God's grace that you have been saved!).

8). God saved you by his grace when you believed. And you can't take credit for this; it is a gift from God.

9). Salvation is not a reward for the good things we have done, so none of us can boast about it.

10). For we are God's masterpiece. He has created us anew in Christ Jesus, so we can do the good things he planned for us long ago.

Because God loves you so much, He wants a real relationship with you. By His grace (which means we don't deserve it—but He did it anyway), He put a desire in you so you would want to know Him. Then, He gave you courage and humility so you could ask Jesus (God) to be Lord... your Lord—over your whole life, trusting that He has a far better plan for your life than you can imagine.

Once you chose Him, He immediately made your spirit alive. Think of it as a sort of spiritual "mouth-to-mouth resuscitation..." God (Who is Spirit) breathed life into your spirit (which had been dead) so that you could be in a relationship with Him. It's "Spirit-to-spirit resuscitation"! Now, just like you have a physical birthday (the day you were born on earth), you also have a spiritual birthday, which is the moment you chose God, and He gave life to your spirit, and you were "born again"—spiritually... Your spirit was made alive to God, by God. And He is with you every moment, working things out so you will see, more and more, how much He loves you and just how very special you are to Him.

As Jesus said in John 3:3-6 (*New International Version*, 2011):

> "Very truly I tell you, no one can see the kingdom of God unless they are born again."

> "How can someone be born when they are old?" Nicodemus asked. "Surely they cannot enter a second time into their mother's womb to be born!"

> Jesus answered, "Very truly I tell you, no one can enter the kingdom of God unless they are born of water and the Spirit. Flesh gives birth to flesh, but the Spirit gives birth to spirit."

# JOURNAL ENTRY:

## 2019 Plan A and Plan B

*Recently, I sought direction for a job. Plan A was where my heart was, and Plan B was where my heart was NOT. I was working out a strategy to keep both options viable since Plan B was one step ahead of Plan A (in that I had not heard back from Plan A yet, but I had heard from Plan B).*

*The Lord cut right to my heart and said, "I don't have a 'Plan B' for your life; why do you need one?" He challenged me, saying, "Either you believe what I said to you and what you spoke out to Plan A, and you're going to take action towards it, or you don't."*

*I was cut to the quick!!! I immediately took action towards Plan A (by packing and selling my house even though I hadn't heard anything from them) and severed Plan B permanently. And, of course, after I stepped out in faith, I heard from Plan A, and the timing was perfect all the way around.*

# CHAPTER 2:

# WHAT DOES "BEING A CHRISTIAN" MEAN?

Becoming a Christian is so exciting; however, I know it can also be a little overwhelming at first, so I'm writing to help guide you in getting to know God and learning how to let Him be your friend and your Lord. Let's look at the Word:

James 2:23: "And the scripture was fulfilled that says, 'Abraham believed God, and it was credited to him as righteousness, and he was called God's friend'" (*New International Version*, 2011).

Exo 33:11a: "The Lord would speak to Moses face to face, as one speaks to a friend..." (*New International Version*, 2011).

And Jesus said in 1 John 15:15: "I no longer call you slaves because a master doesn't confide in his slaves. Now you are my friends since I have told you everything the Father told me" (*New Living Translation*, 2015).

So, what does "being" a Christian mean? What's your next step? What do you do now? Sadly, this is often where well-meaning people step in and give lists of behaviors to correct or modify... things they think you should or shouldn't do: stop smoking, read two Bible chapters every day, stop drinking, pray three hours a day, and the lists go on and on. UUGGHH!!!

I'm not saying you shouldn't read the Bible, pray, or stop doing things that are harmful to you. I'm saying don't get bogged down and busy trying to change your behaviors when God is more interested in you getting to know Him—which is the only way to be genuinely transformed on the inside, which will show on the outside.

Being a Christian is not about having lists of "dos and don'ts" or "behavior modifications." It is about getting to know God personally and intimately; by doing that, we will become like Him. That is our ultimate life goal! Spending time getting to know God and letting His love enter every area of our hearts and lives will always make us more like Him... holy.

My definition of holiness is doing what pleases God and not doing what hurts Him. Holiness in your life is the natural by-product of spending time with God. The more you're with Him, the more clearly you see His love for you, which causes you to love Him more. The more you love someone, the more you want to do what pleases and delights them and makes them happy, and you purposefully don't do things that hurt them or things you know they don't like.

The Bible says in Matt 6:33, "But seek first his kingdom and his righteousness, and all these things will be given to you as well" (*New International Version*, 2011). To "seek first his kingdom" is to pursue His presence, obey Him, and let His will, His plans, and His dreams become yours. "His righteousness" means to be diligent in making sure nothing keeps you from a right relationship with Him.

So, by acknowledging Him, understanding and believing that He is always with you, being consciously aware of His nearness—and interacting with Him—while believing in and receiving His love, you will be able to know the truth about God because you will know Him personally... intimately. Should the enemy attempt to convince you otherwise (i.e., thoughts in your mind saying you're not good enough or lies about God's character by trying to make you think God is "not good" or that He "doesn't love you"), you'll be able to distinguish truth from lies about God because you'll know Him well.

For example, I have walked in on conversations about someone, and because I knew the person, I could say, "I know Bob, and I know his character and heart. He would not do that. Somehow, there has been a misunderstanding because I know he would never purposefully or intentionally do that."

It's just like that with God. You will get to that place in your relationship with Him that when the devil lies about God or whom God says you are (i.e., "You're too much trouble for God" or "How could God possibly still love you after what you've done?" or "You'll never be good enough for God to use you, you'll always be like this, just give up now and walk away... You're too far gone and bad to be a Christian," or "You've been struggling with the same problem for so long, God is done with you, He gave up on you... you're not worth it," etc.), you can tell they are lies because God, Whom you know personally, would never say that. In fact, God says the opposite about who you are and how much you are loved and treasured.

# You Are Loved

Another amazing thing happens when your understanding of God's love for you grows... You are enabled to love Him more—"We love because he first loved us" (*New International Version*, 2011, 1 John 4:19)—allowing you to love others more like He loves them—"Beloved, if God so loved us, we also ought to love one another" (*English Standard Version*, 2016, 1 John 4:11). Our ability to love God and others is directly related to our ability to believe and receive God's love for us. That is the message God wants you to know more than anything... how much He loves YOU!

God only had one Son—Jesus—and He painfully, yet willingly, let him leave heaven to become human and live on the earth (that He created with his own words). Father God let Jesus, and Jesus chose to die a horribly cruel death—as a ransom payment for you... payment for every wrong thought, word, and action you would ever say and do (if you recognize them, confess them, and ask Him to forgive you)—then, after your debt was paid, three days later, Father God raised Jesus back to life—proving Jesus is God's Son, fully God and fully man. He's hoping that when you become aware of what He did for you—out of His great love for you—you would choose to believe and accept His payment for all of your wrongdoings as a gift from Him. While receiving such a great gift of love, you'd respond with love by letting Him be your Lord... in charge of your life to make sure you succeed and make it to the end of your life victorious: guiding you, encouraging you, protecting you, disciplining you, and providing for you.

You'll live your life "for Him and with Him" more and more as you become increasingly aware of how extravagantly He loves you. He did all this with you in mind! He did it so that He could have a deep, genuine, loving relationship with you forever! That's how precious you are to Him!

As He shows you who He made you to be, He also empowers you to be that person inside and out, through and through, the real you. Know this: The real you (the perfect you) already exists in the mind of God because He sees your end from your beginning, and He desires to and knows He can keep you faithful to the end. According to Jude 24-25 (*New Living Translation*, 2015):

> Now all glory to God, Who is able to keep you from falling away and will bring you with great joy into His glorious presence without a single fault. All glory to Him Who alone is God, our Savior through Jesus Christ our Lord. All glory, majesty, power, and authority are His before all time, in the present, and beyond all time! Amen.

So, think of your journey more like you are shaking off, dropping off, and getting rid of all that you are NOT so that the real you—the very image of God Himself that you carry on the inside—can shine through more and more.

# Behavior Modification vs. True Transformation

No matter how great it appears, behavior modification can only last a short time without true inner transformation. Behavior modification is like a coat of paint on a rotten barn; it will wear off in the storms of life, and the rotten barn will be exposed. However, when you change the core of who you are by what you believe about God and about yourself, then what you do will also change. That is a complete renovation from the foundation up, so it will stand strong through the storms.

Your core beliefs, which I define as the "subconscious beliefs that dictate your reactions and responses to everything in life," will change as you spend time with God and listen to the truth of Who He says He is and who He says you are.

Each time a truth settles deep in your core beliefs (replacing the lie that was there), you begin to respond out of that new truth. It's a process! You begin to see you have options, whereas before, like me, perhaps you thought, "That's just how I am."

I consistently reacted the same way, wrongly, and it was so fast that I didn't even recognize I had a choice. My "auto-response" was pre-programmed. However, as the truth settles in, it changes everything.

Transformation is a journey of processes! With every right choice to agree with God and ask for His help and forgiveness, the truth goes deeper into you. It transforms your beliefs until, finally, your core beliefs—"those subconscious beliefs that dictate your reactions and responses to everything in your life"—line up with God's truth and dictate your auto-responses according to what God says is right and true.

A journey of processes might look something like this: God reveals (shows) a truth to you—for example, that you are loved—and then a situation arises—someone rejects you—and despite knowing the truth, you react the exact wrong way you did in the past—sadness and anger... However, a couple of days later you realize you were wrong, and you see clearly where you made the wrong choice to react. You agree with God that what you did was wrong and ask Him to forgive you and help you, and God forgives you. That truth God showed you goes deeper. Then God, in His faithfulness to you and His love for you, wanting to help you be free in this area, provides another opportunity for you... a similar situation. This time, when it arises, you might blow it again, but perhaps you realize it only hours later, instead of days, and you ask God to forgive you and help you... That truth goes deeper. Then, the next time, you might realize it within minutes and ask God to forgive you and help you... That truth goes deeper. This cycle of God providing opportunities for you out of His allegiance to you and His affection for you continues... Then one day, you see your choice right in the middle of the situation, and you can avoid a wrong reaction.

As God's truth is cemented, becoming your new core belief, the tables are turned... You will reach a point where you don't have to make a conscious choice to respond in God's way because now His way is your "subconscious belief that dictates your reactions and responses." His way becomes your new "auto-response." Praise God!

# Understanding Your New Identity in God's Family

When we embrace salvation through Jesus Christ, it's not merely a change in our spiritual status; it's an official adoption into a new, eternal family where God is our Father.

## Adoption Into God's Family

This concept of adoption is powerful. In Roman culture, to adopt someone meant you fully embraced them as your own child, even granting them the same rights and privileges as a biological child, including the right to inherit. This is the picture Paul paints for us in Romans 8:15-17, where he says, "The Spirit you received does not make you slaves so that you live in fear again; rather, the Spirit you received brought about your adoption to sonship. And by Him, we cry, 'Abba, Father.'" (*New International Version*, 2011). "Abba" is an intimate word, just as we would say "Daddy," reflecting a deep, personal, and familial bond.

Understanding salvation as adoption reshapes every aspect of our lives. It tells us we are wanted, loved, chosen, and valued children of God. God didn't just save us; He brought us into His family. This truth should fill us with an incredible sense of security and belonging. No matter our past rejections or hurts, we find a place where we are loved and accepted in God's family.

Rom 8:16: "The Spirit Himself testifies with our spirit that we are God's children" (*New International Version*, 2011).

Col 1:16: "For in Him all things were created: things in heaven and on earth, visible and invisible, whether thrones or powers or rulers or authorities; all things have been created through Him and for Him" (*New International Version*, 2011).

Every person on earth is God's creation, and God loves everyone, always and without any conditions; however, only those who have been born again are "children of God."

John 3:16: "For God so loved the world that He gave his one and only Son, that whoever believes in Him shall not perish but have eternal life" (*New International Version*, 2011).

John 1:12: "Yet to all who did receive Him, to those who believed in His name, He gave the right to become children of God" (*New International Version*, 2011).

As a child of God, you are an heir with Jesus, so all that God is, and all that God has... is available for you and to you, forever!! You get to be in a real, loving relationship with God forever.

# JOURNAL ENTRY:

## 2017 I Choose to Linger

*I've been singing the song from worship (Linger) all morning. Having my quiet time today, I talked to the Lord and squirreled off randomly several times concerning everything on my "to-do" list. Realizing my quiet time was ending, I was gutted and said, "Lord, I don't want to go away from our time feeling like I sat here with my back to You all morning... Lord, I am here; I will linger here with You; what do You want to say today?"*

*Immediately, I saw a picture of me as a child sitting on the floor at His feet with my arms tightly wrapped around His calves and my head pressed firmly as if I were holding on for dear life. Then I saw Him lean over, put one hand behind my back and one under my knees as He lifted me to His lap, and then He wrapped His arms around me. Then I heard Him say, "I'll linger here with you."*

*And I just started bawling as He met me where I was at that moment. He is so thoughtful and knows how to go straight to my heart!*

*(God knows you, and He loves you! Give Him time today to show it!)*

# *JOURNAL ENTRY:*

## *2018 How Can I Please You Today?*

*ME: Lord, how can I please You today? What can I do to put a smile on Your face today?*

*THE LORD: It's not what you do that makes me smile... it's who you are!*

*ME:* 😂😂😂😊😄😄😄😄

# JOURNAL ENTRY:

## 2021 My Word for the Year is Trust

*My word for this year from the Lord is TRUST.*

*In my quiet time this morning, I was excited and pondering it again when all of my strategic thinking started kicking in. And I realized that if it's going to be a year of trusting God more, I will have to have more opportunities to trust Him, which means I will have to be put into more situations where I have a choice to trust God or not.*

*Immediately, I said, "YIKES, LORD??!!??" in a slight panic.*

*God quickly answered: This is a twofold promise to Me this year.*

*Yes, I'll learn to trust Him more, but He said it will also be a year when I'll see the rewards He has for me for the trust I've already demonstrated.*

*ME:* 😂😂😂😂😂 *Yes, Lord... I'm all in!*

**CHAPTER 3:**

# GOD STILL SPEAKS

## The Holy Spirit's Transformative Work

Our transformation process, becoming like Christ, is primarily the work of the Holy Spirit. He refines, challenges, and empowers us to live out the fruits of the Spirit, such as love, joy, peace, patience, kindness, goodness, faithfulness, gentleness, and self-control (Galatians 5:22-23).

This transformation is not overnight; it's the journey of a lifetime in which the Holy Spirit patiently works in and with us to mold us more into the image of Jesus.

Think about when you first accepted Christ and how different you are now. The changes in your desires, your habits, and even how you relate to God and others are all evidence of the Holy Spirit's work in your life.

He is the craftsman of our souls, continually chipping away at our imperfections to reveal the real us... the Christ-like, perfect child of God that He already sees in us. He also fortifies and strengthens us, deepening our capacity for love, humility, and grace.

# Recognizing the Holy Spirit's Promptings

Learning to recognize and respond to the Holy Spirit's promptings is vital for all of us desiring a closer walk with God. His promptings often come as gentle nudges rather than loud proclamations—a sudden thought to pray for someone, an inexplicable urge to read a particular scripture, an unshakable desire to call someone, or even a hesitation that stops us from making a wrong decision. Being sensitive to these promptings means staying attuned to the voice of the Holy Spirit, ready to obey no matter how big or small the guidance might seem.

Let's cherish His presence as we continue to walk with the Holy Spirit. For He is the very breath of God within us, leading us into all truth, comforting us in every sorrow, and transforming us into the image of Christ. Through Him dwelling in us, every moment of our lives is an opportunity to experience and respond to God's love.

## Different Ways God Talks to Us

There are so many ways God can talk to us. He isn't limited at all. Think about the time he needed to get a message to Balaam. In Numbers 22:22-35, you see the story of God using a donkey to speak to him. We can get many ideas of how God can talk to us just from reading the scriptures. Some conversations were out loud dialogues; other times, God spoke to people in dreams or visions, circumstances, angelic encounters, or that still small voice inside our mind. He spoke through His word, nature, and creation, prophets and prophetic words, or through art and creativity, even through our trials and challenges or the wise counsel of others.

The most important concept for you to grasp is that God wants to talk to you, and He knows how you will hear Him (even if it might take a donkey), so you don't have to worry about not being able to hear Him. God will ensure you'll have your moments for leaps of faith. If I were to touch on every one of these formats, this would be a very long book. I am only going to focus on some basics. At the end of the book, I will give you a list of over 150 scripture passages of God speaking in various ways so you can spend time reading and spotting the ways He spoke.

God communicates with people in diverse ways tailored to individual needs and contexts. Here are some of the ways through which God speaks to us:

**Scripture**: One of the primary ways God speaks to us is through the Bible. Scripture provides guidance, instruction, comfort, correction, and encouragement. God's written word teaches us about His character, will, plans, and desires.

**Prayer**: Prayer isn't just about speaking to God; it also involves constantly listening to Him with our hearts and minds.

**The Holy Spirit**: The Holy Spirit is our counselor and guide, dwelling within to prompt, convict, and direct according to God's will. This can often be experienced as a "still small voice" that offers internal direction or understanding.

**Circumstances**: God can use life situations to guide or give us insight. This can include opening or closing doors of opportunity, bringing about significant life changes, or setting up seemingly coincidental encounters.

**Nature and Creation**: God speaks through the natural world, revealing His power, creativity, and the order of His creation. Observing the world's complexity and beauty can lead to greater understanding and revelation of God.

**Wise Counsel and Community**: God can provide guidance and clarity through the wisdom of other believers, mentors, pastors, and spiritual leaders. The Christian community is designed to support, teach, and counsel each other based on biblical wisdom.

**Dreams and Visions**: Some people receive messages from God through dreams and visions. These messages can sometimes be clear and directive or symbolic and require interpretation.

**Prophetic Words**: Prophecy is a significant way through which God communicates. This can involve foretelling future events or speaking about the current circumstances in an edifying, exhorting, and comforting way.

**Art and Creativity**: God can speak through various forms of art and creativity, whether it's music, painting, writing, or other creative expressions. Artistic mediums can convey God's truths and insights in unique and powerful ways.

**Life's Challenges and Trials**: Sometimes, God's voice or lessons come through difficulties and trials. These moments can refine us, teach perseverance, and deepen our reliance on and relationship with Him.

Each method can help individuals discern and understand God's voice and guidance in their lives. It's essential for each person to weigh these communications carefully, ideally against the truth of Scripture and the counsel of wise, spiritually mature believers.

Here are a few conversations to give you an idea of Biblical dialogues:

Exodus 33:11-23: The Lord spoke to Moses face to face like a friend. This conversation is intimate and direct.

Another example is God's conversation with Paul on the road to Damascus in Acts 9:1-7.

In 1 Samuel 1:10-20, Hannah pours out her soul to God, detailing her deep desire for a child, and God listens to her plea and answers with a child.

In Matt chapters 1 & 2, you can read how God used angels and dreams to speak to Joseph about Mary and the baby.

In Genesis, we read about God's incredibly loving conversation with Cain, in which he attempted to warn him. Then, we read about several conversations He had with Abraham.

These conversations aren't just ancient stories but models for our Christian life. They teach us that conversing involves talking to God about our deepest fears and desires and pausing to hear His response, whether it comes as a whisper in our hearts, through Scripture, the wise counsel of a friend, a vision, or a dream while we sleep. The point is that there is always a response from God, even if it isn't immediate.

# *JOURNAL ENTRY:*

## *2023 Sitting With the Lord*

*As I was sitting with the Lord this morning, I was going over the cost of moving and how it just keeps going up and up, and I was getting really concerned. I poured my heart out to the Lord and quickly became grateful for everything He's done to get me this place and work out all the details to move this weekend. Then the thought crossed my mind, "You should ask Him what He wants to say to you," and I realized I'd been talking the whole time, lol. So I started to voice the question out loud, "Lord, what would..." and He blurted out, "I've got you!" That's all it took for me to be completely undone. I cried as His words cut through everything, bringing immediate peace and comfort. I started crying at first because of the words, then realized that God was so eager to comfort me that He didn't even wait for me to finish my question before answering. As a matter of fact, I'm quite sure He's the one Who even put the thought in my head to ask Him because He was so desiring to let me know He was everything I needed in that moment. Our God is faithful = constant in His allegiance and affection to and for us! I pray for a life-changing encounter with God for you today as you read this.*

## Taking Another Leap of Faith

I remember another time in my life when I was so consumed by fear that it controlled what I did. I'd been forced to watch a lot of horror movies as a child, and fear affected me into adulthood. I couldn't take a shower if my roommate wasn't home for fear of what might happen because my imagination would go a hundred miles an hour with all the gruesome possibilities; I couldn't take a shower in a glass stall because I'd seen someone get locked in and scalded to death in a movie. I would lay awake night after night, imagining the most horrific things happening to me. Occasionally, I'd be so overwhelmed with the dread that someone was in my room that I was paralyzed with fear... I couldn't even roll over to look. I remember making the choice one night, while experiencing a moment of paralyzing fear, to turn and lay flat on my back... I folded my arms and put my hands over my heart and, with tears streaming down the sides of my face, I closed my eyes and quoted two scriptures I'd memorized:

Rom 8:15: "For you did not receive a spirit that makes you a slave again to fear, but you received the Spirit of sonship. And by him, we cry, 'Abba, Father'" (*New International Version*, 2011).

And 2 Tim 1:7: "For God has not given us a spirit of fear, but of power and of love and a sound mind" (*New International Version*, 2011).

And I said out loud: "God, I am choosing to believe You, so I'm closing my eyes. Whether I live or die tonight, I choose to trust You. Please put me to sleep." I woke up the next morning, went about my day, and repeated the same scriptures and prayer with tears the next night. I continued night after night for a while until, one day, I realized I hadn't been afraid nor said the verses the night before, nor in quite a while! I could look back and see weeks of no fear! I can't tell you the exact moment, but I can tell you I was set free from fear!!!

To this day, I have no recollection of anything "amazing" happening at that moment... no fireworks, no angels (that I could see), no special feeling, nothing, but I believed God... I took a leap of faith in those moments that carried the weight of life or death in my mind... I chose to live His truth, and I was transformed and set free. Now I know about God's goodness through experiencing it myself.

Eph 3:19a: "[That you may really come] to know [practically, through experience for yourselves] the love of Christ, which far surpasses mere knowledge [without experience]" (*Amplified Bible*, 1987).

A real relationship with God will require leaps of faith on our part. To start with, you must choose to believe that God wants to meet with you and listen to you, talk to you and share things with you, reveal secrets to you, and help you overcome every hindrance, obstacle, and roadblock in the path of your destiny. It is a journey of processes, one choice after the other.

# JOURNAL ENTRY:

## 2018 Put Your Hope in God

*Jer 50:36b: "A sword upon her mighty warriors that they may be dismayed and destroyed!" (Amplified Bible, 1987).*

*As I read this, the Lord showed me that this is one way the enemy attacks us. He works on dismaying us, breaking down our courage, and thoroughly disheartening us in an attempt to make us powerless and ineffective in every area of our lives.*

*ME: PUT YOUR HOPE IN GOD!!*

*Then God reminded me of Phil 4:8 (Amplified Bible, 1987):*

> *For the rest, brethren, whatever is true, whatever is worthy of reverence and is honorable and seemly, whatever is just, whatever is pure, whatever is lovely and lovable, whatever is kind and winsome and gracious, if there is any virtue and excellence, if there is anything worthy of praise, think on and weigh and take account of these things [fix your minds on them].*

*Hallelujah! God always has a path to victory!*

# JOURNAL ENTRY:

## 2023 Weird and Rough and Great!

This weekend was weird and rough and great! Starting Saturday, I was drained... I mean, super weak... I felt 😵😫😖yucky-cruddy and had a nasty headache. Then, it was difficult even to hold my head up Sunday morning. I thought it might be covid, so I wanted to protect my coworkers and get tested before showing up to work on Monday. There's a store 10 minutes away, but the thought of finding parking and having to walk in and find the kit and then stand in line, etc., was just too much, so I opted to drive a little farther, where they'd bring it right out to me in my car. I placed my order and headed out. When I got there, I decided to get gas first. When I say that I felt cruddy, it showed... I'm talking about no makeup, hair sloppily piled on top of my head, a baggy shirt and sweats, 🤪and dark sunglasses because they hide everything 🥸 🥸 🥸 (I did brush my teeth 😁).

As I finished getting gas, I noticed a woman across from me and I happened to glance at her pump. I can honestly say I don't ever remember looking at how much someone paid for gas before, but I noticed she put in exactly $5. And immediately, the Lord said, "pay for her gas." So I flagged her to get back out of her car and asked if I could pay to fill her tank. She was happily shocked and grateful. I felt the word of the Lord stirring in me, so I began telling her how much God loves her, and He sees her right now, right here, and He wants her to know how special and important she is to Him and that He is always with her and thinking about her.

She started getting a little emotional, and I asked if I could pray with her. As I prayed, I knew that something had recently happened that hurt her deeply. So I prayed into that... how God sees it and will heal her, and that He made her heart so He could fix it. I finished praying with her and encouraged her to set aside some time today to talk to Him and tell Him everything. Now, she was very emotional, and she committed to doing that.

I was once again blown away by God's attentive, thoughtful love for this woman (Pearl, in her 30s), that He would make it so that I'd drive all the way there, at that exact moment, so He could tell Pearl how much He loves her. I realized later that I felt better too (and no covid), and by 5 pm Sunday, it was as if the weariness never happened! Praise God ♥

As I drove home, praying for her and envisioning the great things God could do through her, He filled me with the encouraging knowledge that from this moment on, everything He does through her life will also be part of my heritage. WOW. OUR GOD IS ALWAYS SO GOOD!!!

# SECTION 2:

# BUILDING YOUR FRIENDSHIP

# WITH GOD

The most essential aspect of any relationship is getting to know each other. Think of any person in your life you met and had to get to know... Think about the things you did to get to know them... It's the same way with God. You can get to know God in lots of different ways.

The more you get to know God, the more you see He is faithful. You will become more confident in your ability to hear His voice, and it will become clearer and nearer than ever. As you read some of the ways God has spoken to me and others, let it encourage you as to how He can and will talk to you

# CHAPTER 4

# BUILDING FRIENDSHIP

# THROUGH PRAYER

Prayer is simply talking with God. Think about it: The Creator of all that exists, the King of all Kings, the one Who holds the universe together with His Word, eagerly wants to talk with YOU! Remember that He is just as eager to speak to you as He is to hear from you, so remember to give Him time to talk while you listen. Sometimes, the most challenging part of prayer is making time to sit and listen and give God the opportunity to speak. It takes practice.

## Prayer Ideas:

### *In Prayer, You Can Pour Your Heart Out to God:*

1 Pet 5:7: "Cast all your anxiety on him because he cares for you" (*New International Version*, 2011).

#### *JOURNAL ENTRY: 2017 Hiding From God*

*ME: "Lord, sometimes it feels like I'm hiding from You. Looking back, I recognize that it usually happens when I feel like I don't measure up... or I feel that I'm somehow letting*

You down. Thank You for pursuing me with Your goodness and mercy and overtaking me with love."

GOD: (He answered me with a moving picture in my mind, and I wrote it so I'd remember it.) You put Your hand on my shoulder and turned me around. Now, face to face, I see Your arms open wide because the truth is You are always right by my side. I press into You full force, and You wrap me in Your presence.

ME: "You're exactly everything I need... I love You!! When will I learn the full depth of Your love... the height and breadth of Your love... a love so absurd and so captivating that I never have to hide again? Help me to fully live out the victory secured by Your precious Son, Who loved not His own life more than He loved me."

## In Prayer, You Learn He Has Every Answer You Need, Always, at All Times, for Everything:

James 1:5: "If any of you lacks wisdom, you should ask God, Who gives generously to all without finding fault, and it will be given to you" (*New International Version*, 2011).

### JOURNAL ENTRY: Talking a Rough Situation Over With the Lord...

GOD: "When you're tasked with something to do, you have a choice of how you perceive it in your heart and what you wear on your sleeves for others to see—what's going on inside you versus what you show others:

You can choose to wear something as a burden in your heart and on your sleeve. You make sure everybody knows you're doing it, and it is a burden.

*You can make it a burden in your heart, but wear a smile on your sleeve and pretend to be happy doing it... so as not to offend... or maybe it's so you don't look bad?*

*You can choose to make it a joy in your heart but still wear it as a burden on your sleeve... because maybe that gets you more attention.*

*You can choose to wear it with joy in your heart and on your sleeve—and do it rejoicing!*

*Which of these do you think pleases Me and puts a smile on My face?"*

*ME: "Jesus, help me!!! How do I move from the first three to the last one?"*

*GOD: "It's all about GRATITUDE!!! Whether you feel like it or not, you can begin to thank Me for every aspect of your tasks. Thank Me for the fact that you are able, capable, and willing to do it."*

*God gave me understanding: When we see things through the eyes of gratitude, it's easier to be filled with the Lord's joy! Joy in His goodness, joy in His thoughtfulness, joy in knowing He is our source, joy in being in His presence, etc.*

*Neh 8:10b (New International Version, 2011): "The joy of the Lord is your strength" IN & FOR ALL THINGS!*

### *In Prayer, You Can Tell God the Things That Make You Happy and Grateful:*

#### *JOURNAL ENTRY:*

*I'm driving to work and thanking God for opportunities today to be a blessing to my customers through ministry and helping them get their new bathrooms, opportunities to be a* blessing to the company by ministering and selling bathrooms to my customers as the Lord leads, opportunities for me to be blessed financially so that I can be generous on every occasion, etc.

GOD: "Having an attitude of gratitude changes your altitude. It draws you closer to Me, so it's easier for Me to bless you. Besides, being up here with Me, you get a better view."

ME: How do you respond to such thoughtfully extravagant goodness?!?! I immediately started thinking of more things to thank HIM for!

## In Prayer, You Can Tell Him the Things That Hurt You:

Psa 6:6-9 (*New International Version*, 2011):

> I am worn out from my groaning. All night long, I flood my bed with weeping and drench my couch with tears. My eyes grow weak with sorrow; they fail because of all my foes. Away from me, all you who do evil, for the Lord has heard my weeping. The Lord has heard my cry for mercy; the Lord accepts my prayer.

### JOURNAL ENTRY: 2021 Lord, I'm Frustrated and Disappointed.

ME: Lord, I'm frustrated and disappointed.

GOD: You need to realize that the degree to which you are frustrated and disappointed reveals the degree to which you are not trusting Me—not trusting that I'm in control and I've got this, not trusting that I know what's best for you and that I'm working towards that end.

ME: *(although driving to work) Everything in me was bowed in repentance and gratitude. Lord, I trust You; help my mistrust!*

## In Prayer, You Can Ask Him to Help You:

Psa 30:2: "Lord my God, I called to You for help, and You healed me" (*New International Version*, 2011).

Psa 54:4: "Behold, God is my helper; the Lord is the upholder of my life" (*English Standard Version*, 2016).

### JOURNAL ENTRY: 2018

*Driving home from church, all the roads were really icy because of a storm, and it was all back roads to my house. I was going less than 20 miles an hour and still lost complete control of my car three times. That last time was the worst... spinning back and forth and sliding completely sideways towards oncoming traffic. I found myself at that moment screaming in my mind, "JESUS," white-knuckled and holding my breath.*

*I heard Him answer me instantly in my mind: "Okay, turn the wheel to the left and now to the right... When you get to the grass, ease yourself back onto the road... Don't stop." The Holy Spirit talked me through each movement as it was happening at lightning speed. OUR GOD IS SO GOOD!!!!*

## In Prayer, You Can Ask God How He Sees You:

Zech 2:8: "For this is what the Lord Almighty says: 'After the Glorious One has sent Me against the nations that have plundered you—for whoever touches you TOUCHES THE APPLE OF HIS EYE'" (*New International Version*, 2011).

Rom 8:38-39 (*New International Version,* 2011):

> No, in all these things we are more than conquerors through Him Who loved us. For I am convinced that neither death nor life, neither angels nor demons, neither the present nor the future, nor any powers, neither height nor depth nor anything else in all creation, will be able to separate us from the love of God that is in Christ Jesus our Lord.

**JOURNAL ENTRY: 2014**

*ME: "Am I more messed up than I know? Show me how You really see me... I want a true estimation of where I'm at in Your opinion." Then I wrote down what was going through my mind—that I was expecting to hear an answer in the format of a good leader/boss which is "like an Oreo." As a manager, I know how to focus on something positive first, then you bring in the area that needs correction, then you end with another positive. I said again, "God, show me how You see me." This time, it came with tears from deep inside. All it took was a picture to calm all my fears and woes.*

*One simple picture from Him: a perfect—spotless—bride in her beautiful white gown. As you can imagine, I lost it that day, and today, I'm reminded fresh and new that God knows everything and sees the end from the beginning. If He believes in me and sees me like that, who am I to question His ability to complete the work in me? Hallelujah! It's not about trying and trying; it's about trusting and relying!*

# In Prayer, You Can Ask What His Plans Are for You:

Jer 29:11: "'For I know the plans I have for you,' declares the Lord, 'plans to prosper you and not to harm you, plans to give you hope and a future'" (*New International Version,* 2011).

*Psalms 50:23 (The Passion Translation, 2020):*

*The life that pleases Me is a life lived in the gratitude of grace, always choosing to walk with Me in what is right. This is the sacrifice I desire from you. If you do this, more of My salvation will unfold for you.*

*GOD: "When you truly understand My grace, gratitude overwhelms you, causing a deep desire to want to know Me more... to want to be with Me more. And the more time you spend with Me and get to know Me, the more you become like Me... My desires become your desires... meaning... you willingly choose holiness. And as you increasingly choose holiness, I increasingly reveal My salvation plan of FREEDOM, HEALTH, and WHOLENESS in every facet of your being."*

## *In Prayer, You Can Talk to God About Anything:*

### *JOURNAL ENTRY: 2018*

*I'd been singing this line from a song in my mind for two days: "The Cross Has the Final Word." Now I'm driving home and chatting with the Lord, and I just said out of the blue...*

*ME: "What does that mean to you?" (The line from the song)*

*He answered with four simple words that had me bawling like a baby...*

*GOD: "You were WORTH it!!!"*

*I know, right!!! It's so like Him, yet it caught me so off guard that I wept to the point I could hardly drive. I was utterly overwhelmed with His love at that moment!*

# CHAPTER 5:

# BUILDING FRIENDSHIP

# THROUGH SCRIPTURE

Reading God's Word (the Bible) is another way to get to know Him. As you read the different stories, you'll see various people's interactions with God, and it will open your eyes to new ways to learn about Who He is and how you can interact with Him, too. I love reading God's deep conversations with different people because it drives me to want to know Him better and better... to be able to have such in-depth conversations like two friends talking. The Bible is God telling us about Himself, constantly revealing His character, nature, and intense love for us.

You'll read about incredible miracles, touching moments, people living in victory, and people making mistakes. You'll read about dysfunctional families, broken people, and how God helped them. The Word of God is full of the trials, failures, and triumphs of regular people just like you and me. It tells us how God was always there for them and assures us He is always here for us as well.

Every "how to" you need for "life and godliness" can be found in the Bible. But the most important thing for you to know about the Bible is that it's a love letter from God to you. You cannot help but see God's love for you all the way through. Anywhere you read, there is a facet of His love for you and His desire to have a relationship with you being demonstrated.

Throughout the Bible, conversations reveal Who God is and His desires for us. Think about the conversation Jesus had with Nicodemus in John 3 about being born again. Or John 4, where Jesus has a word of knowledge for the Samaritan woman at the well and has a heartfelt conversation with her, even offering her living water to quench her spiritual thirst forever.

These conversations are historical accounts and examples of how God relates to us personally. They teach us about the nature of God. Studying these interactions will help us anticipate how God might respond in our own lives.

## Scripture Reading as a Conversation Starter

When you sit down with your Bible, picture yourself conversing with God. Each passage you read is part of a dialogue where God is ready to speak and eager to communicate with you personally. This approach means you don't speed-read through verses; it involves reading and waiting, listening, ruminating, and responding to what God says. Start by inviting the Holy Spirit to open your spiritual eyes and ears to His voice as you read. Ask questions like, "What are You saying to me today, Lord?" or "How can I use the truth of this scripture in my current situation?" This prayerful questioning and listening will transform your reading time into a beautiful encounter with God.

I highly suggest even memorizing some scriptures. God can give you a strategy of what to start memorizing that's just for you... i.e., verses about how much He loves you, or how amazing He says you are (your identity in Christ), or how trustworthy and faithful He is, or how He will never leave you, or how good He is, or how you are healed and protected, etc.

Memorizing scripture helps you get to know God because you are embedding His character and nature into your subconscious, and it will change the way you view Him.

It has helped me get to know God the Father more personally. Growing up, I didn't have a good father, so when I first read about God as my "Heavenly Father," it didn't sit well with me. My view of "father" had been defined by my own experiences with several not-so-good fathers and father figures.

However, something remarkable happened as I began to read and memorize scriptures about God as a good father. These truths started to sink into my subconscious, gradually changing my core belief about my Heavenly Father. The more I meditated on these scriptures, the more I saw God as a loving, caring, and always good father.

Now, I no longer cringe inside when I hear the word "father." Instead, I feel a deep sense of comfort and love because I know I have a new father Who is always good to me. This understanding has become a fact in my life, not just an abstract idea. Memorizing and internalizing these scriptures has genuinely transformed my perception of and relationship with God, and it can do the same for you.

Here are examples that demonstrate some of the great things God showed me as I read the Bible, how I turned scriptures into prayers, and how I turned what I was learning about God into teachable lessons to help others.

## *JOURNAL ENTRY: 2018 Eph 2:18*

*My scripture from the Lord, on New Year's Eve for 2018, was Eph 2:18. So, I have been reading books, studying the various scriptures, etc. I often said "Daddy" in my prayers, but He wanted me to get a deeper revelation... I learned yesterday that even at my most genuine moments of saying it, I have no real revelation of what "Father" means (because of the abuse* and abandonment in my past)... I have said it more out of faith, hope, and even a little fantasy rather than actual personal knowledge of God as MY Father. The Lord gave me a moving picture. It started with Jesus. I saw Him sitting cross-legged on the floor, and I was lying in His lap, and He reached to pull me closer. Then I heard Jesus would introduce me to the Father... When we turned, there was no one there... just a big yellowish circle blocking the view. I stood up to look for the Father, and someone put their arms around my waist from behind me to hold me. Fear of the unknown gripped me, and my arms and legs flailed about as my head frantically whipped back and forth, from right to left, feverishly trying to see who it was behind me—holding me.

I thought (from the strange comfort that the arms around my waist brought) that it might be the Father, but not being able to see for sure if it was really Him and not knowing what He was going to do with me was disquieting, to say the least. The struggle continued with me desperate to get a glimpse, to know for sure, before I let my guard down and gave up the fight. Then, we moved to the Holy Spirit, and the movie shifted to me as a little girl holding hands with Him, licking a lollipop, skipping, and talking 100 mph.

Suddenly, the Holy Spirit stopped me, and in one swift move, He pulled the Father in His place and put my hand in the Father's hand... I did not pull away; when I looked up, the Father looked just like Jesus. At that moment, John 14:26 and John 14:9 became a real and personal promise to me. Although not without trepidation, I do look forward to the journey.

## JOURNAL ENTRY: 2022 Acts 2:22-25

Acts 2:22-25 (Amplified Bible, 1987):

> You men of Israel, listen to what I have to say: Jesus of Nazareth, a Man accredited and pointed out and

*shown forth and commended and attested to you by God by the mighty works and [the power of performing] wonders and signs which God worked through Him [right] in your midst, as you yourselves know—this Jesus, when delivered up according to the definite and fixed purpose and settled plan and foreknowledge of God, you crucified and put out of the way [killing Him] by the hands of lawless and wicked men. [But] God raised Him up, liberating Him from the pangs of death, seeing that it was not possible for Him to continue to be controlled or retained by it. For David says in regard to Him, "I saw the Lord constantly before me, for He is at my right hand that I may not be shaken or overthrown or cast down [from my secure and happy state]."*

ME: *Wow, God, what an epitaph for Jesus! God, I'd love for You to be able to say all that about me... As I read v. 23, I see that You also had a plan that required tremendous suffering and sacrifice, but then in v. 24 there was liberty as You raised Him from the dead... Lord, help me in my journey of mountaintops and valleys to be like David in v. 25, always recognizing You are with me and around me so that I cannot be shaken, overthrown, or cast down from my security in You and Your love for me.*

## JOURNAL ENTRY: 2020 Exodus 17:9-10

*Exodus 17:9-10 says the warriors attacked them. Moses commanded Joshua to choose some men and go fight for them, while Moses would be standing at the top of the hill holding the staff of God in his hand. So Joshua did what Moses had commanded and fought the army. It struck me that it doesn't say Moses called for Joshua... or sent a search party out for him. It doesn't say Moses said, "Bring Joshua to me," etc.; it says, "The warriors attacked," and "Moses commanded Joshua." To me, that means Joshua had to be right there near him.*

*Exodus 32:17: Joshua was on the mountain of the Lord with Moses.*

*Exodus 33:11: Joshua not only went with Moses to the tent of meeting, he lingered there on his own afterwards.*

*ME: Reading this Chronological Bible, I find it amazing how I see things so differently. I didn't realize the different times and ways it mentions Joshua being with Moses. And then the Holy Spirit just dropped this in my brain: "If you want to be used mightily by God, it's wise to find a leader to serve... and in so doing, you'll also glean from them."*

## JOURNAL ENTRY: 2020 Phil 1:27a

*Phil 1:27a: "Whatever happens, keep living your lives based on the reality of the gospel of Christ, which reveals Him to others" (The Passion Translation, 2020).*

*PRAYER: Lord, You are worthy; worthy to be the focus of my thought life. Please help me be deliberate in what I choose to think about. Let me meditate, ponder, and think about those things that are TRUE and noble and good and upright and holy and of good report. Help me be consciously aware that my attitude is my choice, and out of love for You, I can choose moment-by-moment, day-by-day, and minute-by-minute, the attitude that reflects You, Your true nature, Your true character, Your goodness, and Your passionate love for every person in a way that would draw them to You... that would create a hunger in them to know You... Lord, I choose to live my life focused on You and Your ways, Your plans and Your purposes, and what You are passionate about. Please help me be more aware of Your presence within me, Holy Spirit, and help me live this out in a way that I can fulfill Your purpose for my life for such a time as this!!!*

# JOURNAL ENTRY: 2020 Josh 14:6-15

*Josh 14:6-15: Caleb's confidence in God... 40 years earlier, Caleb, along with Joshua, had given the report full of faith about God's ability to help them conquer the land. Now, 40 years later, Caleb is reminding Joshua about the promise Moses made to him, and he's asking now for the land that was promised to him. It's interesting how he puts the truth in verses 7 and 8 when he says he returned and gave an honest report, but his brothers who went with him frightened the people from entering the Promised Land. Yet, there are no signs of inner struggles with bitterness or doubt in verse 12 when he says (New Living Translation, 2015):*

> *So give me the hill country that the Lord promised me. You will remember that as scouts, we found the descendants of Anak living there in great, walled towns. But if the Lord is with me, I will drive them out of the land, just as the Lord said.*

*This shows that even after 40 years of wandering in the desert (because of his brother's poor decisions), he still had just as much faith and confidence in God and the promise God had given them. The result: verse 13, "So Joshua blessed Caleb son of Jephunneh, and gave Hebron to him as his portion of land" (New Living Translation, 2015).*

*Sometimes, it's easy for us to start grumbling about how long it's taking for a promise to come about, listen to the devil, and start questioning ourselves: Did God really say that to me? Or worse yet, start doubting God's ability and goodness to bring about what He said He would do.*

*How long does it take before we throw in the towel or start trying to make it happen ourselves? One year? Five years? Ten years? Caleb believed God at his word FOR 40 YEARS, and as a result, he says in verse 11, "I'm as strong now as I was when Moses sent me on that journey, and I can still travel and fight as well as I could then" (New Living*

*Translation, 2015). God had kept Caleb until the promise would be fulfilled.*

*Lord, I believe You at Your word and trust You to bring about every promise You've given me! I choose to put my hope in Your goodness to keep me until You bring every promise to fruition! In Jesus' name, amen.*

## JOURNAL ENTRY: 2021 Mary and Martha

*Mary and Martha: I just realized I had based my entire opinion of Martha and Mary solely on one recorded moment in scripture... Luke 10:38-42: Martha tells Jesus to make Mary help her, and Jesus says Mary has chosen the better. God forgive me and help me!*

*Martha (and those of us who tend to be driven, multitasking, goal-oriented, high-capacity operatives) has gotten a nasty rap most of the time. However, I saw something new and fresh that was so exciting. First, when you read that passage, you'll see that Martha was so welcoming that Jesus accepted her invitation to come for dinner.*

*John 11:5-6: "Now Jesus loved Martha and her sister and Lazarus. So when He heard that Lazarus was sick, He stayed where he was two more days" (New International Version, 2011). WAIT... WHAT?!? Jesus, knowing His friend Lazarus was sick, knowing Lazarus' family (whom he stayed with 11 times in Bethany—Martha & Mary) needed Him, He decided to WAIT TWO EXTRA DAYS before going to them? Why would God do that? Verse 4 tells us why: "When He heard this [Lazarus was sick], Jesus said, 'This sickness will not end in death. No, it is for God's glory so that God's Son may be glorified through it'" (New International Version, 2011).*

*John 11:20-32 (New International Version, 2011):*

*20) "When Martha heard that Jesus was coming, she went out to meet Him, but Mary stayed at home."*

So, this is what struck me... in the midst of their struggle, disappointment, grief, etc., Martha, as soon as she heard Jesus was near, went to Him, poured out her heart to Him, worshiped Him, and declared her faith in Him. Mary stayed in the house in her grief and disappointment. When Martha went back and pulled Mary aside and told her Jesus was asking for her, she went out, but what she said sounded like she had no hope and was disappointed in God... It almost sounded like perhaps she was even blaming God.

32) "Lord, if You had been here, my brother would not have died." That is quite different from Martha's statement in verses 21-27:

> 21) "Lord," Martha said to Jesus, "if you had been here, my brother would not have died.
>
> 22) But I know that even now God will give you whatever you ask."
>
> 23) Jesus said to her, "Your brother will rise again."
>
> 24) Martha answered, "I know he will rise again in the resurrection at the last day."
>
> 25) Jesus said to her, "I am the resurrection and the life. The one who believes in Me will live, even though they die;
>
> 26) and whoever lives by believing in Me will never die. Do you believe this?"
>
> 27) "Yes, Lord," she replied, "I believe that You are the Messiah, the Son of God, Who is to come into the world."

So, KUDOS to Martha!! And questions for us: How do we respond when things don't go how we think they should, or how we want them to, or at the time we think they should? What is your auto-response when things don't go your way *or seem to go wrong? Are you like Martha: go to God, pour out your heart, worship Him, and declare your trust in Him? Or do you question God's character or nature—that He is good? Do you question His Word or His love for you? Or do you perhaps even blame God? Only God knows our hearts. No matter if your auto-response is more like Martha or Mary (in this one recorded moment in scripture), God's love FOR us doesn't change; however, if we let it, His love will change us.*

## JOURNAL ENTRY: 2020 2nd Timothy 1:13-14

*2nd Timothy 1:13-14 (The Passion Translation, 2020):*

> *Allow the healing words you've heard from me to live in you and make them a model for life as your faith and love for the Anointed One grows even more. Guard well this incomparable treasure by the Spirit of Holiness living within you.*

*Lord, help, show, and teach me how to allow the healing words I've heard from You to live in, dwell, and transform me. Help me believe everything You've spoken to me, so much so that my entire life is transformed. Jesus, as my faith in You and my love for You grows more and more, let Your words become the model of my life!*

*Help me live out every dream, plan, and purpose You have for my life. Enable me to choose to think and act rightly so that I live out the destiny You desire for my life. Holy Spirit, thank You for living in me and being my teacher, helper, guide, comforter, and encourager. Thank You that I can trust You to help me hold on to these truths... to guard them and keep them at the forefront of my consciousness so that my thoughts and actions reflect Your truths. In JESUS' NAME, AMEN!!!*

# JOURNAL ENTRY: 2022 Job 42:7-10

*Please read the whole thing first, then join me as I break it down with what the Holy Spirit showed me. It was so cool reading Job again. I can't help but bow my heart afresh every time I read the part where God questions Job regarding all that exists. But this time, I was extremely moved by the verses after that. It's so like the Holy Spirit to make something I've read so many times suddenly captivate my attention with revelation and insight like never before.*

*Job 42:7-10 (English Standard Version, 2016):*

*a) OK, it says that "after God finished speaking to Job, He said to Eliphaz..." So, God spoke straight to Eliphaz. It doesn't say that He told Job to tell him or anyone else. GOD SAID, "I AM ANGRY WITH YOU AND YOUR TWO FRIENDS." I see this picture of God whipping His head around suddenly to Eliphaz and blurting that out. YIKES... You wanna talk about getting "the look"? I think they got "the look"!!!* [Lord, help me and forgive me and teach me Your ways.]

*b) But why was He angry? "for you have not spoken accurately about Me, as My servant Job has." God was angry because they misrepresented His character and nature.* [Lord, help me always represent You to the best of my abilities. Let my life and my speech truly express Who You are and how good You are!]

*c) God is bragging about Job. He says "my servant Job" in every sentence, four times in a row, making a strong point to them of how highly He personally regards Job.* [Lord, help me live my life so that when the time comes, You can brag about me... "Well done, good and faithful servant"]

*d) Then God tells these men they must go to Job (the one they just accused of all kinds of evil) "and offer burnt offerings for themselves," utterly humbling them.*

*e) Then God says, "My servant Job will pray for you, and I will accept his prayer on your behalf." Ouch! Not only do they have to go to Job with an offering, but they also must get Job to pray for them... Their lives depend on it.* [God, help me be quick to repent when You prompt me and walk in humility, confident of Your goodness when I obey.]

*f) Then God lets them know He is going to extend grace: "I will not treat you as you deserve" but...* [Lord, thank You for not treating me as I deserve! Thank You, Jesus, for trading places with me.]

*g) He is REALLY not happy about them misrepresenting His character and nature. If you think I'm kidding, read it again... He repeats Himself—for the second time in four sentences!—"for you have not spoken accurately about me, as my servant Job has."* [God, help me be the very best ambassador possible for You.]

*h) So they obeyed and went to Job, and the Lord accepted Job's prayer. I put myself in their shoes... hmm... I just spent all this time accusing Job of evil, and now God Almighty is angry with me because I blew it big time and made Him look really bad in all of my accusations, and my only hope is that Job won't hold it against me... that he'll forgive me and intercede for me with God?* [Oh, Lord help me!] *I think I would be bawling, puking, and I don't even know what else. I would be so scared and shaking in my boots, a nervous wreck. I know there would be a part of me that took solace in the part where God said, "I will accept his prayer on your behalf," but I don't know if I'd be calm and cool regardless.*

*i) One of the most beautiful verses in this book to me is verse 10: "When Job prayed for his friends, the Lord restored his fortunes." Let's face it: Job could have been mad and bitter at them; if you read v. 8, it says, "Go and offer a burnt offering." What if Job rejected their offering? There are 42 chapters of reasons he could use to justify not forgiving them. These are his friends, and they tore him to shreds! On the one hand, God said, "My servant Job will pray for you," but let's be real, there are many things Job could have prayed that just might not have been God's "best." The truth is that we don't know precisely what Job prayed, but his heart must have been right because God blessed him with double after he prayed for them.* [Holy Spirit, help me be quick to forgive, loving towards all You've made, pure in my thoughts and intentions, and faithful in serving You and Your people!]

## The Timeless Truth of Scripture

Keeping scripture at the forefront of your mind throughout the day can transform ordinary moments into God-encounters. One practical way, as I mentioned earlier, is through scripture memorization. Start with one verse a week, reciting it during your daily activities—while waiting in line, exercising, or even doing household chores.

Technology offers handy solutions, too. Consider using a Bible app that features daily verses or allows you to listen to audio Bibles. Listening to scripture while you commute or begin your day can be a powerful tool for consistently building your relationship with God.

## Journaling as a Response

Journaling is a powerful way to record what you hear from God through scripture. It lets you document your thoughts, revelations, prayers, and actual dialogues with God. This practice helps clarify your thoughts and creates a log of your spiritual journey you can revisit to see not only how God has spoken to and led you over time, but also the growth in your life. I never would have imagined that all these journal entries would be part of a book, but God knew. I'm learning so much while writing this book and revisiting some of the lessons I journaled long ago. It's like a refresher course. It's incredible to see how much I've changed—and still need to change—in some areas and, most importantly, to see God's faithfulness to me throughout the years as He continues to hone my spiritual hearing and my relationship with Him.

Start by making a note of the scripture you're reading. Jot down any words or phrases that stand out, and write down your thoughts and what you believe God is saying to you about it. You can jot down how it applies to your life. I even write down my prayers to God about what I just learned and ask Him to help. Journaling like this will turn your reading time into a documented dialogue that can continue to speak to you days, months, or even years later. And who knows... It could be the fodder for your own book down the line.

By approaching scripture with the mindset that it is an opportunity for conversation, you open your heart to hear God's voice more because you're expecting it. This practice takes your reading from a routine exercise into a powerful interaction with the living God. His words are alive and active, ready to penetrate your heart and transform your life. As you continue to assimilate these practices, the living Word of God will dwell richly within you, blessing you in every way as you walk with Him.

# JOURNAL ENTRY:

## 2017 Be Real and Heal, or Keep Going

## Around This Mountain?

GOD: I'm giving you a choice right now: either be real and heal or keep going around this mountain.

ME: Well, God, that sounds easy, but being real means showing all my ugliness right now. Really, God? Seriously? In my second week at this new church? You want me to alienate leadership by exposing myself as a "fear-of-man" driven, people-pleasing, prideful (we all know, because we have heard it for years, that insecurity is still pride—still focused on self—just on the negatives instead), pitiful, needy, broken little sheep? That's the part of me You want them to see first? Whatever happened to putting my best foot forward? How will I ever get back into full-time ministry if this gets out and that's what people think of me?

GOD: Do you want to heal? You keep asking Me to search your heart and cleanse you, so I am telling you now... you need to work on this! You will not alienate them; this is why I have you here. They are strategically placed right here for you right now! You can no longer keep the things you don't like about yourself bottled up for fear of being seen as "less than." If you continue to hide your wounds, they will fester, and you will rot from the inside out. Some wounds depend on exposure to heal.

ME: But God, how on earth am I going to walk up to someone and just tell them all my crud? I have no idea how it would be received or whom I would even share it with. You said I have to be responsible about whom I share what with. I'm sure most people don't just do that; it could really set me back as far as Your plan for my life regarding prophetic worship because I'm certain they will not let someone this psychotically insecure on stage to help lead others into Your presence. (bawling) God, how can You ask me to do this? This will ruin everything! You told me to come here and join their worship to learn more facets of You and now You are asking me to throw it all away?

GOD: Do you really think I would ask you to throw it all away? Do you really think I would ask this of you to hurt, or harm, or humiliate you?

ME: (still bawling) No, Lord, I don't!

GOD: I know you don't!

ME: Lord, I'm scared! (now profusely bawling) Whom would I share it with? Holy Spirit, I need Your help. I need You to show me the right person with the character, maturity, and integrity to see this situation as You do and respond how You know I need. God, even though all I can foresee is disaster, You know I trust You, and I'm going to obey You... ☺ You've known all along, and You're so patient in talking me through this epic freak-out.

ME: Spontaneous worship and gratitude.

# CHAPTER 6:

# BUILDING FRIENDSHIP

# THROUGH WORSHIP

## Worship as a Lifestyle

Most people equate worship to singing songs in church, but let me tell you that worship is so much more. It's an expression that not only happens in musical moments but in every decision made according to God's will, and every act of love and obedience is an act of worship to God. We can actually create and live out an entire lifestyle of worship. Simply put, a lifestyle of worship is a choice of our will, moment by moment, to do what we know is right and pleasing to God. Whether you're working, spending time with your family, or out having fun, approaching it with an intention to reflect God will turn everyday living into worship. It's about making your whole life a testimony of His goodness and sovereignty.

How, then, do we create a lifestyle of worship? We start by learning to declare God's greatness from our mouths. Faith comes by hearing and hearing by the Word of God. Declaring and decreeing biblical truths about God's nature and character actually help change us and build our faith in God and His goodness. Isn't that so like God? We worship Him, and we reap benefits. I love how thoughtful He is. As we get to know Him more through worship, we are drawn closer to Him, so we get to know Him even more, which produces the next level of worship. It's a beautiful cycle that will continue until we are in heaven with Him forever. I'm reminded of how it says the angels never cease worshiping God. I think it's because they constantly see new facets of Him that ignite a whole new level of worship every time they turn around.

I want to share some tips on where and how to start incorporating worship into your daily life. Hopefully, you'll see how worshiping God can bring greater intimacy to your relationship with Him.

# The Power of Perception

Tenney once illustrated the power of worship beautifully. He described looking through a magnifying glass at a grasshopper, noting that as the magnifying glass was pulled back, the grasshopper appeared larger, though it hadn't actually grown. Tenney explained this is what happens when we worship: God doesn't get bigger, but our perception of Him does. Worship pulls back the "magnifying glass" of our perspective to enlarge our view of God. We begin to see the truth of how incredulous He is and what the God of the universe, Who is our friend and our protector, our healer, our comforter, our guide, and our strength, can do on our behalf. With that in mind, we love Him more for it, so we respond in that newly increased love.

# Expanding our Worship Vocabulary

One of my greatest joys is giving away these flashcards I make with some of God's attributes listed to help expand worship vocabulary. Simply put, an attribute is a trait that's built into someone. It's a part of who they are. These cards are designed to be easily memorized or carried and read often.

I had to study God's attributes when I went to college (2013-2016), which changed my life—so much so that I began my own campaign to bless others. I learned that my brain is limited with what it can think up on the spot when it comes time to worship. My heart was ready to express my worship, but the same words were the only things that would come to mind: "You are good," "You are faithful," etc.

Have you ever said some words so much that they almost lost their meaning to you? Someone taught me the power of recognizing that our minds are computers. If I give my mind a task, everything in me goes to completing that task. If you've read my first mini-book, *The Proverbial Tongue*, you know about using the alphabet to get our minds on task computing so we are free to worship. I highly recommend the alphabet worship tool; however, these cards are my favorite by far, and as I said, I love to give out sets. I've probably made and given out about 200 sets to date.

My goal is to teach you how to expand your perception of God easily so you can continue and even get creative with your own new concepts and ideas. Please don't be limited to what I am sharing; this is just your starting point. It's your turn to take it and run with it, just like I did with what she shared with me.

# Memorizing and Meditating on God's Attributes

Memorizing and meditating on attributes of God is a powerful practice. Reflecting on God's nature anchors our core beliefs in His unchanging character rather than our own ever-changing circumstances. For instance, when we get into a situation we can't control, we can remind ourselves of and meditate on God's sovereignty. That will help us remember to trust Him, knowing that He's working things out for our good. Memorizing these attributes allows us to recall them during quiet reflection and in the rush of everyday moments, transforming our mundane moments into spontaneous worship times.

## Attributes of God

Here are several attributes, including the words from each flashcard I created, for you to meditate on and talk to God about. You can ask him to reveal these attributes to you and even help you understand each one more so you can know him more and be re-inspired to worship Him. He loves those kinds of prayers.

### God is Omniscient:

God knows everything possible to know;

therefore, He never needs to learn anything!

He knows the past, present, and future of every

creature that ever was, is, and ever will be!

God is perfectly acquainted with every

detail in Heaven, on the earth, and in hell!

Nothing and no one anywhere, ever, can

escape His notice or be hidden from Him!

God sees, hears, and knows all at all times, so

nothing and no one is ever forgotten or overlooked

by Him! His knowledge is without limits, so He can

never be surprised or caught off guard!

## God is Omnipresent:

God is always everywhere at the same time.

He is Spirit, so He can be in all places at once!

Where could I go from Your Spirit? Or where

could I flee from Your presence? Psa 139:7 NKJV

If I ascend up into Heaven, You are there; if I make

my bed in Sheol, behold, You are there! Psa 139:8 NKJV

There is nowhere in Heaven, on the earth, nor under

the earth where men can hide from God's presence!

He is infinite, so there is no limit to His presence;

therefore, there is no place beyond His presence!

## God is Omnipotent:

God has all power to execute all of His will at all times!

His Power is infinite, eternal, and unlimited! Because

He is Self-Existent, and His Power will never run out!

God's Power is not acquired and, therefore not

dependent on anyone or anything outside Himself!

God is the source and originator of all power!

There is absolutely nothing He is unable to do!

No prayer is too big or too small, no

need too great or unimportant,

because He is self-controlled and still

generous in exercising His Power!

## *God is Love:*

God not only loves, but He is Love; therefore,

He always wills good towards all of creation!

God is Eternal; therefore, His Love has no beginning

nor an end, and neither does it have limits!

His Love is self-sacrificing in that He willingly

chose to lay down His life in exchange for ours!

God's Love is passionate, emotional, active, and

unconditional. It can't be earned nor escaped from!

God's Love takes pleasure in us—the chosen objects

of His affection, & He holds no good thing from us!

His Love is uninfluenced by anything; therefore, He

always does what is highest & best for all of creation!

## *God is Eternal:*

God is the Alpha & Omega, the Beginning & the End.

Nothing was before Him nor will be after Him!

He existed before all of creation and will be there at the end!

Eternity is the very essence and nature of God; therefore,

He's not subject to the measurement of time!

Time dwells in God; therefore, there is no

past, present, or future in eternity!

Rev 4:8 Holy, Holy, Holy is the Lord God

Almighty, who was and is and is to come!

## God is Holy:

God is utterly separate & set apart from sin, & He is

the perfect embodiment & sum of moral excellence!

God is absolute purity in Whom there

is not even a shadow of turning!

Isa 6:3 "Holy, Holy, Holy is the Lord of Hosts;

the whole earth is full of His glory!"

God's Holiness can be seen in His Word, words,

precepts, works, laws, decrees, and statutes!

I believe the greatest manifestation of His Holiness

(& love) is what He did for us by way of the Cross!

God is infinitely perfect in righteousness, so

everything He does is right, pure, and holy!

### God is Good:

God is Immutable, meaning He cannot and does not change. Therefore, He is always good at all times! God's Goodness inclines Him to be kind, benevolent & full of goodwill to mankind & all of creation! His Goodness is eternal, perfect & self-caused; therefore, it is not provisional, nor can it be swayed by anyone or anything! There is nothing we can say, pray, or even do to earn salvation; it is a gift from God out of His Goodness! Every good and every perfect gift comes from God. We don't deserve it, and we can never repay Him! We are to walk in the "Fear of the Lord," yet in His Goodness, He teaches us not to be "afraid" of Him!

### God is Faithful:

God is Immutable, meaning He cannot and does not change. Therefore, He could never be unfaithful! God is steadfast, unwavering, and never fails in His allegiance and His affection towards us! God is always true to His Word, His promises, and His vows! God can be believed & relied upon. His Faithfulness is our shield & buckler: Our means of defense & protection!

God's Faithfulness can be seen in His invariable

loyalty, trustworthiness, and devotedness towards us!

## *God is Sovereign:*

God is infinitely elevated above the highest of

creatures; He alone created all that exists!

He is Lord of Heaven and Earth, so He is subject to

neither anyone nor anything except His Word!

God is absolutely free to do as He pleases, with all

authority to carry out all His will at all times.

No one and nothing can hinder or thwart God's

will and plans because He is always in control!

God is seated on His throne in Heaven, directing

all things and working all things as He wills!

## *God is Self-Existent:*

God stands alone as being uncreated

and Creator of all that exists!

Nothing or no one caused God to come

forth. He has no origin of beginning!

"I am the Alpha and the Omega, the Beginning

and the End," says the Lord God,

"He Who is and Who was and Who is to come,

the Almighty" (the Ruler of all)! Rev 1:8

God requires no source outside of Himself

to sustain Himself except Himself!

God is Self-Controlled, Self-Sufficient,

Self-Reliant, Self-Contained, and Autonomous!

May your friendship with God deepen as you grow in your understanding of Who He is and how much He loves you, and may this knowledge lead you to a greater awareness of His presence in your life.

# Stock up on Ammunition

What's incredible is that once you memorize them, they become ready ammunition in your worship arsenal. Start by memorizing just one card, and you will be amazed at how those words flow out so readily during your private and corporate worship times. We have to tell our brain to begin, and then all the work we put in to memorize pays off when we no longer have to strain to think up great things about God. You've loaded your computer program with the pertinent info, and it will do its job when you tell it to.

It's life-changing to have so many true and personal things to say to God and about God.

Whenever you want to.

# The Power of Worship

Both personal and corporate worship are essential in nurturing our relationship with God. Personal worship involves those intimate moments when you're alone with Him—maybe you're in your car, in a quiet nook at home, or simply on a walk. These are precious times for us to express our adoration to God, our dependence on Him because He's trustworthy, our gratitude for all He's done, etc. It can be in talking, singing, or even expressing our love creatively. There are no limits. It's often when God speaks into the depths of our hearts as well, revealing more of Himself and His will for us. Corporate worship, on the other hand, involves coming together with other believers to worship God. This corporate experience unites us with fellow Christians and helps us see facets of God we might miss on our own. The shared stories of God's faithfulness, the joint singing of His praises, and the united hearing of His Word will enhance our understanding and experience of Who God is.

In the midst of life's trials, maintaining a posture of worship can deepen your relationship with God. It's about leaning into what you know to be true about God's nature, even when circumstances challenge those truths. Consider the stories of Jonah, who wrestled with God's commands, and Job, who endured unimaginable losses. Both faced great trials, yet their stories are incredible examples of how we can respond to our own struggles. It's crucial in these times to focus on God's unchanging attributes—His goodness, His justice, His omnipotence. Even when you're in pain, singing a worship song can shift the atmosphere, turning mourning into dancing and despair into hope. This act of worship doesn't ignore the reality of suffering, but chooses to declare that God is good, even in the midst of it.

By embracing worship as a way of life, you allow every day to be an opportunity to see God magnified and His will performed in your life, and His love declared to you and through you. Whether through song, service, or simple daily acts, let your life praise God Who is worthy, and you'll see the shift in your level of intimacy with Him because He said He inhabits the praises of His people.

# JOURNAL ENTRY:

## 2022 Fun Time With God

*Yesterday, I stepped up from doing physical therapy for the last couple of months to working out on my equipment TWICE!*

*Needless to say, I'm feeling it this morning! So I'm moving slowly but I'm very happy and playful while bantering with the Lord. As I got ready to work out today, I said, "Lord, that movie* Legally Blonde *was right when they said: 'Exercise produces endorphins, endorphins make you happy, and happy people don't kill their husbands...' Soooooooooo, does this workout count as premarital counseling for me... for when You bring my husband?" At that, I burst out laughing and felt Him laughing with me.*

*I believe intimacy with God is not only those private times we set aside to meet Him alone in an isolated place; it's the constant awareness of His nearness every moment of our lives. That comes by consciously acknowledging and including Him in everything. And it takes practice!!!*

# CHAPTER 7:

# BUILDING FRIENDSHIP

# THROUGH AN ATTITUDE

# OF GRATITUDE

There's a simplicity in gratitude that often escapes us. It's like breathing—essential yet mostly unnoticed until we pause and focus on it. I remember vividly when God made the importance of gratitude crystal-clear to me. Think back to my conversation with God, which I shared earlier: God said, "Having an attitude of gratitude changes your altitude. It draws you closer to Me, so it's easier for Me to bless you. Besides, being up here with Me, you get a better view." This powerful statement dramatically shifted my perspective into focus. ~~Gratitude isn't just about saying "thank you"; it's an attitude that transforms us, elevates our spirit, and deepens our relationship with God.~~

Embracing an attitude of gratitude means recognizing our choice and choosing thankfulness in every situation in our daily existence. It's about recognizing every good thing, no matter how small, as a gift from God. This recognition doesn't come automatically; it requires practice, especially on difficult days when gratitude seems like the furthest thing from our minds.

# The Alphabet as a Tool

I've found that the same method we discussed using in worship—using the alphabet—is also particularly effective as a framework for gratitude. Start with "A" and find something to be thankful for that begins with this letter, perhaps "autumn leaves" or "another day of life." Continue through each letter until you reach "Z." This exercise challenges you to think creatively and helps you reflect on many blessings, deepening your appreciation for God's presence in every part of your life.

These practices of gratitude have a direct effect on our spiritual altitude. They lift us from the gravity of negativity and self-focus, aligning us with God's perspective. From this vantage point, the challenges we face seem smaller, and the possibilities for our lives seem endless. Gratitude opens our hearts to see God's active hand in everything, which, in turn, opens the door for more blessings—not necessarily as material wealth or perfect health, but as a richer, fuller, deeper awareness of His presence in our lives.

As you integrate gratitude into your life, expect a transformation in how you perceive your circumstances and experience your relationship with God. Gratitude turns what we have into enough and more. It turns sorrow into joy, fear into faith, and feeling alone into an incredible encounter with God. An attitude of gratitude can help make sense of our past, bring peace for today and all it entails, and even help create the vision of victory for tomorrow.

In a world that often urges us to want, be, and do more, gratitude says, "I am enough, and I have enough," because God is enough. Let this truth fill each day as you live out a lifestyle of gratitude, transforming your walk with God and elevating your relationship to new heights.

As this chapter closes, may your heart remain open to the countless gifts around you, each one a statement of God's love and faithfulness. Embrace gratitude fully, and watch as it reshapes your life, drawing you closer to God and the abundant life He promises.

# CHAPTER 8:

# BUILDING FRIENDSHIP

# THROUGH SACRIFICE

## Sacrifice of Fasting

Fasting isn't just skipping meals—it's about quieting life's noise to hear God more clearly. When you fast, you awaken a deeper spiritual hunger, not just physical. It's about removing life's distractions to focus on God and grow closer to Him.

Clearing away life's clutter through fasting makes space for fresh encounters with God. Moses, Jesus, and the early church fasted during pivotal times, showing that it prepares us for spiritual breakthroughs.

If you're new to fasting, start small—skip a meal and spend that time in prayer. As you get comfortable, you might extend your fasts. Fasting enhances your spiritual sensitivity and prayer life, making God's voice more distinguishable.

Approach fasting with a clear purpose—whether for guidance, deliverance, or deeper worship. It's a sacred time to connect more closely with God, not a way to earn His favor. Think of it as a secret feast with the Lord, a time to enjoy His presence and hear Him more distinctly.

# JOURNAL ENTRY:

## 2022 The Only Response to Love

*ME: Lord, thank You for this breakfast. Thank You for today, a day that You made just for me. Thank You that I'm the apple of Your eye and I'm always on Your mind...*

*GOD: (Instant swoosh like a cloak around me, His presence and love now tangible.)*

*ME: (Now bawling because I recognize that even as I say it, a part of me feels almost guilty, as if it were pride to say those things.) Lord, how can I declare these things and temper them so I don't move into pride?*

*GOD: Keep saying it until you truly believe it, because the more you truly believe it... the more it will humble you. There can be no other response to this truth.*

*ME: (Now really bawling...) Lord, I believe, help my unbelief! Thank You for loving me, thank You for choosing me, thank You for taking the time to teach me, thank You for Your patience with me, especially when it seems like I'm questioning Your character and nature by not fully living the truth of Your love for me. Help me live in light of Your love so I can be a blessing on every occasion today.*

## Sacrifice of Time

Picture taking a break just you and God, away from the daily rush, to connect and refocus. That's what a personal sabbatical is about—an intentional time to deepen your relationship with God.

The purpose of a personal sabbatical is to help you hear God more clearly by removing daily distractions. It's a time to reflect on where you are spiritually and where you want to go, and to listen to God's voice without interruption.

A personal sabbatical can rejuvenate your spirit and bring new insights, which are often missed in everyday chaos. It's a fantastic way to seek direction, heal emotional wounds, or refresh your spirit. This sacred time is a break from life's chaos and a deep dive into your relationship with God by putting Him as your center focal point.

# CHAPTER 9:

# BUILDING FRIENDSHIP

# THROUGH COMMUNITY

## Corporate Worship: Enhancing Our Personal Friendship With God

Surrounded by the voices of fellow believers, our personal friendship with God is not diminished but amplified. Corporate worship—be it through song, prayer, or giving offerings—allows us to experience God's presence in a unique and powerful way and also the truth that "For where two or three are gathered together in My name, I am there in the midst of them" (*New King James*, 1982, Matthew 18:20).

This shared worship experience helps to deepen our individual connections with God. Corporately singing a worship song can often unlock our hearts in ways private worship can't.

This is where our personal friendship with God can grow nourished by every shared expression of faith.

# Learning Together: Fostering Growth in Friendship

The teachings and sermons we absorb in church are not merely educational; they transform us. Communal learning experiences are vital because they challenge our interpretations, invite questions, and provide clarity, helping us avoid the pitfalls of solitary interpretations that might lead us astray.

As we learn together, we find that our growth is interconnected. Your insights can open new avenues of understanding for me and vice versa. This dynamic is one of the Church's greatest strengths. It reminds us that while our relationship with God is personal, it should not be pursued in isolation. We need each other! It's impossible to do life with God without doing life with each other because we see facets and reflections of God in others that we would not see otherwise. The shared experiences within the church walls will enhance our understanding of Who God is and how He moves in our lives, drawing us closer to Him and each other.

# Community Prayer: Strengthening Our Connection With God

I love listening to other people's prayers at church. I always learn something new about God by how others interact with him in prayer. When we voice our concerns, hopes, and thanksgivings together, we are reminded that we are not alone in our struggles or our victories. Praying together binds us to God and each other as we begin to see His heart expressed through their prayers. It allows us to share in each other's burdens and celebrate each other's victories.

In these moments, we often witness God's responses first-hand. We see prayers answered; we feel God's peace and grace reinforce our faith, heighten our understanding of God's character, and deepen our connection with Him. These shared moments teach us about the power and heart of God, Who listens to and cares about our concerns, and they remind us of His sovereign ability to work through every situation for His glory and our good.

# Fellowship as Spiritual Nourishment

Fellowship is crucial because it reflects God's love through human relationships. It provides a support system that upholds us in our weaknesses and celebrates our strengths with us.

In these relationships, we can see God's love in action. A shared meal, a comforting conversation, or a helping hand in times of need—all these acts of fellowship reveal facets of God and strengthen our friendship with Him by showing us His love being lived out. They remind us that He designed us not just to believe in Him but to live out that belief in community, where we can both experience and express His love directly and indirectly through the kindness and care of others. We can express His love to those around us so that they now see a facet of Him they wouldn't see otherwise.

Every one of us reflects unique facets of God that are vital for where we are at this moment in time. There are no accidents. We are who we are and where we are in our lives and all our spheres of influence by God's master design for eternal purpose.

# Sharing Your Journey: Testimonies are Powerful

There's something incredibly moving about hearing someone share their personal stories of friendship with God. Each story is a testament to God's loving intervention on our behalf, and sharing these experiences isn't just about recounting facts—it's about inspiring hope and faith. When I decided to write this book, it was with this mindset. My deepest desire was to share the journey God and I have walked together, hoping with my whole heart that my stories would awaken you more by encouraging and inspiring you to seek after more of your own deeper encounters with God.

When you hear how someone else has experienced God's love, guidance, or even correction, it doesn't just increase your knowledge about God; it enhances your faith by shedding fresh light on Who He really is through someone else's eyes. It makes God's presence more tangible by reminding you that He is actively involved in our lives today, not just in biblical times. It naturally elevates our trust in God's ability to do the same in our own lives. This is why sharing our journeys is so crucial—it bridges the gap between knowing something in our head and living it out in real life.

Eph 3:19 (*Amplified Bible*, 1987):

> [That you may really come] to know [practically, through experience for yourselves] the love of Christ, which far surpasses mere knowledge [without experience]; that you may be filled [through all your being] unto all the fullness of God [may have the richest measure of the divine Presence, and become a body wholly filled and flooded with God Himself]!

# Building a Community of Friends With God

(Rom 12:4-5, Act 2:42, Matt 18:20.) You can hear the Word of God spoken and taught and be around other Christians at church. We become like those we hang around, so get around people whose lives you admire or are inspired and encouraged by. We are created as interdependent beings, which means we were made to need each other. We are all made in God's image; however, each of us reflects a different facet of God. It's a great time to listen to others talk about what God is doing in their lives and share what He is doing in yours so that we can encourage and help each other. (1 Thes 5:11, Heb 10:24-25, 2 Cor 1:3-4.)

Finding or forming a small group focused on spiritual growth and accountability can also enhance your relationship with God by providing a space for more intimate fellowship than what you might experience in larger church settings. They allow for deeper discussions, personalized prayer, and an environment where you can be open and honest about your struggles and victories. Start by contacting your church community to see if existing groups align with your needs, or consider starting one with a few like-minded individuals. The key is to ensure that the group remains Christ-centered, fostering an atmosphere of Bible-based living and encouraging each member to grow in faith. Finding or forming a group may require patience and initiative. When looking for a group, seek one that values transparency, humility, and a desire to see every member grow in their relationship with God.

If you decide to start a group, set clear expectations about the group's purpose, the commitment level expected from members, and the core activities such as Bible study, prayer, and fellowship. Establishing a regular meeting schedule that respects everyone's time while providing enough frequency to develop strong relationships is also essential.

# *JOURNAL ENTRY:*

## *2018 God's Mercy and Thoughtfulness*

*A little over a month ago, the Lord asked me to transition to a different campus at the church where I was (basically) interning. I was going through a painful time, so in talking with the Lord, I said, "Lord, I know what I believe You're telling me, but I need a word from You that is irrefutable, so there's no question later on that it had anything to do with my emotions."*

*God showed me a picture in my mind of a caterpillar over my current location—which turned into a cocoon—that then moved over to the new location as a butterfly burst out. He said, "Now it's time for you to fly." I shared that word with both my then-current leader and my soon-to-be new leader. With their blessing, I made the transition.*

*A while later, on my way to prayer one day, I was pondering circumstances and questioning myself because I didn't seem to fit in anywhere yet. I arrived quite early and sat in my car as my mind swirled with thoughts: "I'm not as eloquent in my prayers as everyone here," "I don't worship the way they worship," "They are all up on current world events, and I am clueless," etc.. Having completely forgotten about the word of the Lord a month ago, I began to question if I had missed the Lord in transitioning.*

*Suddenly, I was reminded that I had an unopened message on Messenger, and the Lord prompted me to open it right now. Below is a recreation of the picture God had someone send days ago, knowing He would ask me to open it today. The person who sent it wasn't a close friend and certainly not anyone who would've known the conversation I'd had with God a month ago! Only God!*

*All I could do was bawl. I went into that prayer meeting overwhelmed with a new awareness of God's goodness and intimate fellowship. I was so moved by His attention to detail in my life and how patient and kind He is with me. He didn't beat me up for letting the devil bombard my mind and forgetting the word He'd given me a month ago; instead, He just lovingly reminded me of it. That's our God—so gentle, so personal, unwavering in His affection, always loyal and steady in His allegiance! HE DOES NOT WANT US TO LOSE EVEN ONE BATTLE!!!*

**give     yourself     time**

# CHAPTER 10

# BUILDING FRIENDSHIP

# THROUGH MATURITY

## Invitation to Deeper Intimacy

Have you ever felt a stirring within you, a pull towards deeper waters in your spiritual journey? I am guessing that is probably one of the reasons you're reading this book. Perhaps during a moment of prayer, a church service, or while reading scripture, something within you whispered, "There's more."

This is the voice of God, inviting you to dive deeper into a relationship with Him, to move beyond the familiar shallows into greater depths of His love and presence.

The phrase "deep calls to deep" from Psalm 42:7 captures this beautifully. It speaks of a deep, echoing call that resonates with the deepest parts of our soul. God is calling us to not just wade but plunge into a deeper intimacy with Him, where we are acquainted with His acts and truly get to know Him personally.

This deeper calling invites us to experience a relationship with God in a way that transforms us.

# Sharing Deep Intimacies With God

In any deep and intimate relationship, sharing your deepest thoughts, fears, and desires is crucial. With God, it's no different. He invites us to pour out our hearts to Him, not because He needs information, but because He desires communion. He already knows everything about us, yet He delights in hearing us share our innermost thoughts and feelings. This sharing is an act of trust and vulnerability that draws us closer to Him.

When we share our deepest selves with God, we acknowledge His lordship over our lives and our dependence on Him. Keeping a journal where you write letters to God expressing your thoughts and emotions and record His responses can be helpful. Think about any close relationship you have and recall times when you shared your deepest deep with them and how that time of sharing drew you closer in the relationship; It's the same with God. This practice helps articulate what's on your heart and serves as a record of your spiritual journey. Reviewing these journal entries, you'll see how God has moved in your life, answered prayers, and drawn you deeper into His love. I love reading David's heartfelt prayers in the psalms.

As we continue to explore what it means to mature in our friendship with God, remember that each step deeper into His presence is a step into greater revelation, transformation, and intimacy. He's calling you deeper, and as you respond, you'll discover not just more of Him but more of who you are in Him.

Go ahead. Right now, take three minutes of gut-level honesty with God about whatever comes to mind.

# JOURNAL ENTRY:

## 2022 To Know to Do Good

*So, I went to heat up lunch in the microwave at work, and someone's reddish something had EXPLODED all over the inside... I set my bowl with its cover in the center (being very careful not to touch any part of the microwave 😄 😷 😅), then, when it was done, just as carefully, I retrieved my bowl and turned to head back to my office... I didn't even get one step, and the Lord said, "To him who knows to do good and doesn't do it, to him it is sin" (New International Version, 2011, James 4:17). 😳 😅 I said, "Yes, Lord," set my bowl down, and proceeded to scrub the microwave.*

*It was a beautiful reminder that God is always with me to help me be more like Him. I am so grateful He takes the time (and has the patience, LOL) to hold me accountable when I'm not living the truth I know. He is able to keep us faithful to the end.* ❤️

# CHAPTER 11:

# FRIENDSHIP BY

# OVERCOMING BARRIERS

## The Challenge of Modern Busyness

Have you ever lived one of those scenarios where you were so excited to go meet up and hang out with a friend, and then as soon as you get there and start to talk, your phone rings, their alarm goes off for some task that must get done now, you hang up and start to talk and their phone rings. Work is emailing, family is texting, and calendar notifications are pinging. Before you know it, the time of deep connection you wanted was fragmented and now over. We have to be careful not to let the pace of modern life hinder or disrupt our time with God.

We can be so busy working for God that we neglect our time with Him. This busyness isn't just about a packed schedule; it's also about the mental load we carry, the constant noise that fills our minds even when we do find a moment to pause.

This impact on our spiritual life is detrimental because we are living beings, so we have only two options: grow or die. If we're not growing, then we are, in fact, dying. Without intentional pauses to be with God, our sensitivity to Him can become shallow, limited to rushed prayers or the occasional church service. We must be diligent not to turn our relationship with Him into another task on our checklist and keep it the life-giving friendship it's meant to be. But here's the good news: God understands and gently calls us to come to Him. It's for our best and highest good, and He's eager and excited to meet with us, knowing He has everything He knows we'll need for what is ahead in our day.

# *JOURNAL ENTRY:*

## *David's Solution*

*Psa 94:19: "Whenever my busy thoughts were out of control, the soothing comfort of Your presence calmed me down and overwhelmed me with delight" (The Passion Translation, 2020).*

*I love David's solution to everything this life throws at us— God's presence!*

## Intentionality in Seeking God

Recognizing the need to connect with God intentionally is the first step towards overcoming the barrier of busyness. He is the life we need for survival and sanity. It requires us to look at our schedules and priorities and make deliberate choices. Sometimes, this means saying no to good things to make room for the best thing—time with God. It might mean waking up a bit earlier, carving out time during a lunch break, or turning off our devices for a period each day to quiet our minds and hearts before God. Strategically, it involves setting appointments with God, much like we would with anyone important in our lives. These appointments aren't just slots in our planners; they're sacred times we guard because we value our relationship with God. They're consistent, non-negotiable times we commit to, regardless of how we feel or what pressing tasks loom. This isn't about legalism; it's about love— a response to the love God shows us and a recognition that we need this time with Him to thrive.

# JOURNAL ENTRY:

## 2017 Journey to Freedom Continued

There are battles I lose to the temporary supposition that what the devil says is true. He uses a voice with an air of familiarity... It sounds similar to mine. Were it not disguised, I would recognize his tormenting tyranny immediately. He bombards my mind with his twisted and distorted version of my circumstances as he assigns his "why" in another attempt to run me down the mental rabbit hole I had frequented so much in the past it became like a second home. He proclaims that these circumstances are more "real" than God's words spoken to me concerning His plan and purpose for my life.

Then, Holy Spirit captures my attention, making me aware of His nearness. In His presence, the tormenting comes to a screeching halt as He brings clarity—through the mind of Christ—that I am where He wants me and that His timing is perfect. He assures me that not one jot or tittle of His plan and purpose for me has changed, and He reminds me that I can trust Him. Awwww... All is good again.

ME: Lord, I'm grieved that I lose so many battles of the mind... However, I'm elated that I can visibly see that the losses are becoming fewer, farther apart, and not so epic. Battles of choice: to believe at that moment what the enemy would call "the reality of my circumstances" or choose to believe You at Your word and hold on to hope. Oh, that it was that simple to see so clearly the choices before me when choosing... For now, while I grow, I'm grateful for having 20/20 hindsight, but I long for and believe in 20/20 foresight.

Thank You, Lord, for putting it in my heart to want to be with You. Thank You for patiently showing me where I made *wrong choices and then teaching and enabling me to make the right ones. Thank You for Your steady allegiance to me in Your willingness to reveal how I got to believing wrong things about You and about myself that would cause me to doubt, even for a second, Your genuine, passionate love for me.*

*You are Truth, and You permeate my whole being when I am with You, reminding me that You have dreams for my life, as a good father does, and that everything You do is for an eternal purpose... Not one moment of my life can be wasted since You are my King, and You have ordered my steps and written out my days. I trust You!!! Your people are my people, so endue me with all that is necessary to be Your hands and heart to those You have placed in my path. May they encounter You through me.*

*You help me lower my guard, little by little, as I get to know more of the real You... Those lapses in my core belief system become sporadic and infrequent until they are completely eradicated, and I will always have 100% confidence in Your reality for my life.*

# Practical Tips for Quiet Time

## *Environment*

Creating an environment where you can give God your full attention is vital to the ease of consistency. Choose a time you can commit to and stick to it. Make sure you choose a place you enjoy and look forward to visiting for your quiet times. If you pick somewhere that is not pleasing, it can weigh negatively on your mind when you're ready to have your time with God.

Choose a place that is free from people or anything that could distract you from God. You want an environment that is conducive to prayer. Otherwise, it becomes easier to make excuses not to meet with Him. Believe me when I say the devil will use anything he can to keep you from meeting with God, so don't give him any ammunition. You must be strategic and intentional in eliminating distractions, even if that means getting noise-canceling headphones (lol).

Set timers or reminders on your devices or sticky notes around your home if needed. Set yourself up for success by being prepared ahead of time. Think about it like this: It's much easier to get ready when you've set your outfit out the night before. It takes longer to get ready if you're still looking through everything, trying to determine what you'll wear while hustling and bustling to get ready.

So, know when you're meeting with Him, know where you're meeting with Him, and have your Bible, journal, to-do list, and anything else you'll need ready to grab and go when it's time to meet with Him. Using aids like prayer journals can also help keep your thoughts organized and focused. I like to have a journal to write down what I say to Him and what He says to me. Begin your time by asking the Holy Spirit to help you focus and speak to you. His role as your guide and comforter includes aiding you in your quest to draw nearer to God.

## *Have Supplies Handy*

Have something to write on so that as things come to your mind, you can write them down and tend to them later. That way, your mind can continue with the Lord instead of trying to remember it all.

Having writing tools helps me because everything I need to do that day often comes flooding into my mind and can distract me from God. I write every task down as it comes to mind, then I can let it go and focus again on God... If I don't write stuff down, it all just keeps going in circles in my mind (because I don't want to forget it), which makes it impossible to focus and give God the attention He deserves.

Not everyone is like me, so you do what works for you. Get creative, think outside the box, and don't limit yourself to what I'm writing... Remember, this is just a starting point or stepping-stone. God made you unique, and He loves how you do YOU!

Just like our human relationships, our ability to hear God and recognize His voice gets better and better. Think about a mother who can pick out her child's cry across the room despite the chaos of many other children, or with only one word spoken over the phone, you know immediately who's calling... (Before we had Caller ID, LOL.) That's how it will be with you and God. As you spend time getting to know Him, you'll begin to hear even His faintest whispers.

Along with our regular time with God, remember that we can talk to Him everywhere, all the time, about everything:

1 Thess 5:17: "Pray continually." He is always with us.

Deut 31:6: "Be strong and courageous. Do not be afraid or terrified because of them, for the Lord your God goes with you; He will never leave you nor forsake you."

Deut 31:8: "The Lord Himself goes before you and will be with you; He will never leave you nor forsake you. Do not be afraid; do not be discouraged."

Matt 28:20: "and teaching them to obey everything I have commanded you. And surely I am with you always, to the very end of the age."

Josh 1:5: "No one will be able to stand against you all the days of your life. As I was with Moses, so I will be with you; I will never leave you nor forsake you."

Isa 41:10: "Don't be afraid, for I am with you. Don't be discouraged, for I am your God. I will strengthen you and help you. I will hold you up with my victorious right hand."

## Technology

Another practical tip is to use technology wisely—set your phone to "do not disturb" or use an app that helps you structure your prayer time. Sometimes, I start with reading the Word, which captures my focus and pulls me into the awareness of God's nearness.

Incorporating these elements into your life isn't about following a rigid formula but deepening your connection with God. It's about making space in your life for dialogues where you speak and listen, transforming your prayer time into a two-way conversation that nurtures your soul and your relationship with God. As you continue to embrace these practices, may your encounters with God be more and more life-giving as they deepen.

## Meeting Time

I suggest setting aside a regular time to meet with God every day. Being consistent is the easiest way I know to make a lifelong habit. If you don't purposefully make God your priority, the enemy of your soul (the devil) will gladly supply many opportunities for busyness and distraction throughout your day until there is no time left for God. We will always MAKE time for what we believe is important. God can put the desire to meet with Him in your heart. One prayer I pray is, "God, help me want to want more of you."

There's nothing you can't go to Him and talk about because He already knows everything. He loves spending time with you! Be sure to make it a two-way conversation. Think about how you might feel if every time a friend comes to see you, they talk the whole time, and you never get a word in. I find this to be the hardest but most satisfying challenge. Believe that when you talk to Him, He will talk back; when you ask Him something, He will answer you. Be open to all the different ways He might be trying to speak to you. He is a good father Who wants you to hear His voice.

His answer might be a picture that comes to your mind (like the pictures I shared earlier of the perfect, spotless bride and the picture of Him turning me to face Him and hug Him), or it may be an idea that comes to your mind that solves your problem (like the song that came to my mind when I needed it); maybe you hear Him talking in your mind, or perhaps you suddenly realize there's something you're doing in your life that hurts God, and now you want to live differently (see Deut 6:18 and 1 John 1:9). That is the Holy Spirit (God) talking to your spirit. The key is to trust God when He said His sheep know His voice; so, as a Good Shepherd, He will speak to you in a way He knows you can hear Him.

## Have Fun and Change It Up

Mix it up when you spend time with God! You can read the Bible, chat with Him in prayer, sing your heart out, or get creative with painting or drawing. Maybe just sit quietly, write, color, or even craft something if you feel like it. I can't say enough about keeping a journal, too! Write down your chats with God, any neat ideas you get, or even answers to stuff you've prayed about. This journal will become a real treasure for you, showing your journey with God.

## Engaging With Scripture Creatively

When it comes to the Bible, don't be afraid to get artsy! You could paint or sculpt scenes from the Bible or create music that makes the ancient stories relevant. You could also write stories or make videos. This isn't just fun—it makes the Bible really come alive, helping you feel and understand it on a whole new level.

# *JOURNAL ENTRY:*

## *2021 Look at You, My Dearest Darling*

*SOS 1:15: "Look at you, my dearest darling, you are so lovely! You are Beauty itself to me. Your passionate eyes are like gentle doves" (Passion Translation, 2020).*

*As I was reading through the first chapter, this verse stuck out. I read it over and over. My heart wanted to bless someone with this word of the Lord today, so I scrambled through various people in my mind (and phone) who I could send it to to encourage them, and no one seemed to fit. Finally...*

*ME: Holy Spirit, this is so good and so powerful... Who do you want to say this to today?*

*As I sat back to wait for names, I heard a huge resounding answer:*

*GOD: YOU!!!*

*ME:* 😂😂😂😂😂😊😊😊😊😊😊😊😊😊😊😊😊😊 😊😊😊😊😊😊😊😊😊😊😊😊😊😊😊😊

# JOURNAL ENTRY:

## 2018 My Journey to Freedom

Have you ever felt like you made the most horrific first impression? Instead of taking time to build stronger relationships with those I connected with in a new environment, I basically vomited my most immature, insecure, wounded thoughts and perceptions about something that had just happened. I was in the middle of processing a situation with the Lord (emotionally, mentally, and spiritually) when the need to share seemed to overwhelm me.

The Lord showed me that insecurity operated in a couple of different ways:

An excessive desire to fit in and be accepted resulted in unfiltered projectile vomiting of my thoughts and emotions in a warped subconscious attempt to cultivate intimacy in the relationship.

He showed me I was looking for a human to fulfill the role that only He could, as protector and healer, to stop the pain.

The Lord is faithful and gave me the clarity and healing I needed. However, now I was bombarded with the tormenting realization that I had completely sabotaged myself in this new environment.

ME: Lord, I blew it! That's just not who I am.

GOD: Were you faking it?

ME: No! But that's just a tiny percentage of who I am, and now it's all they know. They think that's who I am as a whole.

*GOD: Are you willing to look the fool to let Me heal you?*

*ME: (now bawling) Yes, Lord, I am all in—at any cost!*

*As the days progressed, I realized the mental torment regarding what I'd done seemed to be growing, not dissipating. EVERYTHING IN ME WANTED TO FIX THIS!!! To explain: "That's not the real me," "That's not the sum of who I am," "It's just one of my worst moments," "I am more than just a 'boo-hoo Barbie.'" I wanted to say or do ANYTHING to set the record straight!*

*Despite the torrent going on inside, I knew better than to say anything to anyone other than the Lord this time.*

*ME: Lord, I know that how I'm feeling and the constant thoughts I'm having about all the ways to "fix" this are wrong, but I can't put my finger on what exactly is wrong. Holy Spirit, help me! Show me what is going on in me!*

*He told me to text my bestie for prayer. As I pulled her up, I saw something I had sent her a while back.*

*The Holy Spirit said, "Open it." They were meeting notes a pastor had sent me from a staff training session. It was exactly the answer to my question, explaining in detail what was going on in me!*

*A PARAPHRASED SAMPLE FROM THE NOTES:*

*"The spirit of fear is a negative prophetic spirit that gives us a false picture of our future. It causes us to make decisions based on fear, which God cannot honor.*

*Like deciding to have conversations with people because we're afraid we've been misunderstood, saying yes to things because we're afraid to miss out on other opportunities that might be connected, building relationships with 'the right people' so that it will be easier for God to open doors for us (because we don't trust Him to do it), any decision made because we are experiencing fear.*

*Any time we are 'triggered' and try to make that 'feeling' go away by any human means, we act in fear, and the results cannot be good, even if we feel better temporarily, because we are not trusting God.*

*However, any time we act in faith, which requires completely trusting God, the fruit will be good, our future will be secure, and even misunderstandings will fuel God's good work in our lives."*

*I cried out again to the Lord and asked Him to help me.*

*ME: Lord, thank You so much for showing me what is happening; now I need Your help to stop it! I know You have a specific strategy for victory for me at this exact moment. Lord, what can I do RIGHT NOW to win back my mind?*

*Immediately, the Lord dropped a song in my mind, and I began to sing it. Suddenly, I realized the lyrics were the exact answer to my question! It was an old song... "Put on the Garment of Praise for the spirit of heaviness, lift up your voice to God, pray in the spirit and with understanding oh magnify the Lord."*

*As this revelation hit me, I began to pray out loud—in the spirit and with my mind—and praise and magnify God. It wasn't just a couple of minutes, and that overwhelming desire to "fix" everything was gone... just like that! The enemy has tried to bring that fear and humiliation back a couple of times, but now I am armed with the knowledge of his tactics and a specific strategy from God, so I am NOT losing those battles anymore!*

*It's brought a whole new level of trusting God. To be able to rest in the truth that whether or not His plan includes "fixing" this situation, I can trust that He's at work on my behalf and that His plan is for my best. With this newfound trust also comes a joy deep inside inexplicable! Hallelujah! Highest praise to God!!*

# CHAPTER 12:

# OVERCOMING FEELINGS

# OF UNWORTHINESS

Have you ever felt like you're just not good enough for God? Maybe a shadow of past mistakes haunts you, whispering that you're too flawed to be loved by God. Or perhaps a sense of inadequacy creeps in when you compare your spiritual life to others who seem more "holy" or "together." These feelings of unworthiness are not just common; they're also one of the most substantial barriers we face in developing a deep, personal relationship with God.

God, I believe, help my unbelief!!!

## Roots of Unworthiness

It's essential to work with the Holy Spirit to find out where these feelings stem from, as they can often be traced back to specific areas or events in our lives. Sometimes, our past sins are a significant source. We look back on mistakes we've made and somehow allow the enemy to convince us these errors have marked us permanently unworthy in God's eyes. We believe the enemy's lies, which aim to keep us bound in guilt and shame. Another source could be tragic or traumatic events in our lives, such as abuse, neglect, loss of a loved one, etc. These incidents can leave us believing the lies of the enemy— that it is our fault, that something is wrong with us, etc.—and guilt and shame steer us away from God instead of towards an intimate relationship with him. Still, another source could be our tendency to compare our spiritual journeys with that of others. In an age of social media, where everyone's best life is on display, it's easy to feel like our spiritual life doesn't measure up.

We have to remember, too, that the enemy is also determined to distort our perception of God's character and nature. If we have a wrong perception of God, we are far more likely to run from Him than to Him. If we view God as a harsh judge, it'd be easy to feel unworthy every time we fail, and that can make us shy away from God instead of turning to Him. But if we know He's a loving father, then our failures can be seen as opportunities for grace and growth. It's crucial we confront these feelings head-on, recognizing them as barriers to our intimate friendship with God.

# God's Unconditional Love

Perfect love casts out fear—fear of not measuring up, fear of being broken, fear of rejection, fear of abandonment, fear of being hurt, fear of not being good enough, fear of... ????. God's perfect love is the antidote for unworthiness.

Let me say it again: The antidote to feelings of unworthiness is a deep, personal revelation of God's passionate unconditional love for you. The *truth* is, God's acceptance of us isn't based on our perfection but on His grace. He demonstrated that when Jesus died for us while we were still sinners (Romans 5:8). This act of ultimate love was for broken, imperfect individuals—like you and me.

God's love is relentlessly pursuing us for our own good. There is nothing we can do to make God love us more or love us less—He loved us enough to die for us while we were at our worst. His love doesn't keep score of our wrongs or withdraw from us when we mess up. Instead, God's love covers a multitude of sins and empowers us to become the people we were created to be. Embracing this love means letting go of our self-condemnation and self-focus and begin accepting that we are passionately loved, and deeply cherished, flaws and all.

# Scriptural Affirmations of Worth

The Bible is filled with affirmations of our worth and God's love for us. Isaiah 43:4 states, "You are precious in my eyes and honored, and I love you" (*English Standard Version*, 2001). This is a direct statement of our value to God, not because of anything we have done but simply because we exist. Another powerful truth is found in Psalm 139:14, where David speaks of being "fearfully and wonderfully made" (*English Standard Version*, 2001). This scripture reminds us that our very creation was an intentional act of God's love, not a cosmic accident.

Zephaniah 3:17 tells us that God rejoices over us and renews us in His love. Imagine that—the Creator of the universe singing over you full of joy! These scriptures aren't just nice thoughts; they are the reality of how God sees us right now and always. When feelings of unworthiness try to overwhelm us, these are the truths we can stand on.

# Steps to Embracing God's Acceptance

Accepting God's love and overcoming feelings of unworthiness require a strategy from God and the partnership of the Holy Spirit. It's crucial to engross yourself in the truth of God's Word regularly. Habitually read and meditate on scriptures reaffirming your worth and God's love for you. Write them down, memorize them, decree them out loud, and let them replace the lies of unworthiness in your mind.

Another practical step is to practice receiving God's love in your quiet times. Ask Him how He feels about you, and then sit back and listen, or be attentive as you read the Word, expecting Him to speak to you. Allow Him to speak to your heart, and as He does, you'll find that His love starts to heal those deep-seated feelings of unworthiness.

It's also helpful to have honest conversations with mature, trusted friends or mentors about your struggles with unworthiness. Bringing these feelings to light often takes away much of their power. These friends can also remind you of the truth of your worth to God.

Lastly, learn to forgive yourself. God has already forgiven you, if you've asked Him to, and He wants you to forgive yourself, too. If God Almighty says He forgives you, then who are you to say you are unforgivable? Holding onto past mistakes only prevents you from moving forward and accepting the fullness of God's love for you. As you practice these steps, you'll create new habits and thought processes, and you'll find that the barrier of unworthiness becomes less formidable, allowing you to step into a closer and more confident relationship with God, one where His love defines you, not your imperfections, wounds, or past mistakes.

# SECTION 3:

# MORE CONVERSATIONS TO

# PONDER

I'm adding several more journal entries for you to read as added inspiration. I hope my transparency inspires you in a "leap-of-faith" way as you read.

# CHAPTER 13:

# MORE JOURNAL ENTRIES

## JOURNAL ENTRY: 2017 Small and Shortsighted Goal

WARNING: This is probably the most personal thing I have ever posted; get comfy if you choose to read it. I pray it helps and blesses you!

*God does not have a "plan B" for our lives! That would mean that His "plan A" failed, and God does not fail. We are exactly where He knew we would be for such a time as this. God is sovereign and omniscient; therefore, there is nothing we can do to thwart, delay, or mess up His plans for us. He knows the past, present, and future of every living thing, and He knew everything we would ever do, good and bad, every choice, every action, from before time began. He planned accordingly to get us here now, always with the ultimate end-time goal of purifying us to be the holy, spotless, and perfect bride worthy to marry His Son Jesus.*

*I feel I have been preoccupied lately with wanting to get "to doing what I'm called to do long-term." I recently began moving forward in some things God asked me to... one of which was taking piano lessons. My shortsighted focus was made clear to me as my last piano lesson was an EPIC FAIL! I couldn't do anything my teacher wanted me to, and my mind was having trouble forgetting what little I knew from the past (chords, letters, etc.) and learning the new way things are done (numbers). Then, pouncing on my insecurity, the devil bombarded me to the point I was questioning things I've known for years about my calling.*

*The devil said: "You need to stop being selfish and trying to live out these fantasies in your mind. Stop worrying about yourself and just pour into this next generation. Worship teams nowadays are for young people. Nobody will want an old lady singing with them, especially one your size, and who walks as funny as you do. Give it up already. You are just embarrassing yourself at your age. You missed the boat. You missed your chance. Your time has come and gone. You should have done more years ago. Besides, you've got to face facts about your voice... If only one person in your life said something bad about your voice, that would be one thing, but all your life? Those people cannot all be wrong!" Then he reminded me of things said about my voice: "Your voice is different, doesn't blend, not enough vibrato, too much vibrato, too loud, too harsh, not the right sound, not a soloist voice, too country," yada-yada, etc.*

*I didn't even recognize it as the devil at first; I meditated on these thoughts as if they were my own. God, in His great love and mercy, met me where I was and reminded me WHO HE IS! Out of that time spent with God and Him faithfully feeding me the truth, I realized just how small and shortsighted my goal was. No, my struggle is not over, I've had to fight like never before to hold on to the dream God put in me, only now my dream is not so shortsighted and much clearer. I don't have this completely under control, but I know Who does, and I trust Him, so I press on!*

*God's end goal is not to get me into prophetic worship leading to the nations, but to purge me of everything that hinders His love so that I can respond with my voluntary love with no hindrances and let Him sanctify me, purify me, wash me, make me new, remove every spot, every blemish, every wrinkle and prepare me to be presented as holy on my wedding day, a bride befitting the King of Kings.*

# JOURNAL ENTRY: 2014 Being God's Love Expressed

*The Waiter:*

*I went out to dinner and started talking with my waiter. It turns out he moved here to go to Bible College. I was his only table, so he got to sit down, and we chatted. I prayed for him, and the Lord gave me a prophetic word for him. I went back to the same restaurant the following week with a friend, having completely forgotten about that incident. He saw me, came over, said hi, and said he'd told all his friends about me (lol), and they all wanted to meet me... "Can they come over to the table?" I said "absolutely!" Three of them came over with him, and the Lord gave me a word for each one of them. (One of the young men cried as I gave the word to him.)*

*The Postal Worker:*

*I thought I had a free afternoon, so I lined up a bunch of tasks to get done, including a safety inspection for my car. I ended up getting to go to work, and I had about ten extra minutes (beyond what I needed to drive), and I really felt compelled to go home... I was only a couple of blocks away. As I drove home, I saw the mail truck heading down the road towards my house. I pulled in and stood in the driveway, waiting for her to put the mail in my box, and I would go grab it. Instead, she drove right up to me, handed it to me, and said hi, and I said hi... and the next thing that came out of my mouth was absolutely God. I said, "Is there anything I can pray for you?" I don't know who looked more shocked, her or me LOL.*

*She said, "Yes, my husband is really struggling with some health issues right now." So we held hands while she was sitting in the truck. I prayed for her, and she was visibly moved. I was in awe at God that He would have me drive all the way home for just a couple minutes because He loves her and her husband so much He wanted His will prayed over their lives. I'm awestruck as God continues to unfold His goodness.*

## JOURNAL ENTRY: My Moses Moment

*Okay, so this happened tonight... I'm going to call it a "Moses moment" (not my finest moment, admittedly...). I was driving and talking to the Lord about some teaching opportunities that might be coming up, and I found myself trying to convince Him how unqualified I am and how much I don't know. The Lord just cut right in and said, "Good teachers teach out of what they know... GREAT teachers also teach out of what they hope to learn." Hhhmmmm... I've been ruminating on it for hours.*

## JOURNAL ENTRY: Bring Me the Sacrifices I Desire

*Psa 50:14 (The Passion Translation, 2020):*

> *Why don't you bring Me the sacrifices I desire? Bring Me your true and sincere thanks, and show your gratitude by keeping your promises to Me, the Most High. Honor Me by trusting in Me in your day of trouble, cry aloud to Me, and I will be there to rescue you.*

*I never thought of it like this before. The Word commands us to be thankful "for" everything and "in" everything... but I never considered that a sacrifice. Now I see it so clearly... The struggle to choose to be grateful, to keep my promise to trust Him, when I don't understand what's happening and why it's happening is a sacrifice God desires. By taking control and reminding myself of His nature and character, His history of goodness and faithfulness to me, and His promise to always be the same yesterday, today, and forever. To think and speak the truth of His Word until my emotions line up with* the truth... That is honoring Him. To cry out for help, BELIEVING He will be there to rescue me is HONORING HIM.

Lord, please forgive me for the times I have dishonored You and hurt Your heart by not trusting You. Thank You for Your mercy, grace, and patience in teaching me to trust You. I long for and look forward to the day when there is no longer a struggle to choose because trusting You has become my first response, my first inclination, my subconscious natural way of life, and my modus operandi for everything in my life! IN JESUS NAME, AMEN!

## JOURNAL ENTRY: 2017 The Simplest Situations

Holy Spirit, You are absolutely incredulous! You take the simplest situation and turn it into a life-changing revelatory truth!

I woke up this morning overwhelmed with gratitude and yet dissatisfied at the same time. He reminded me of a recent event in which I desperately wanted to sew a button onto a garment for someone. I had searched my entire house but to no avail. I finally just said, "Holy Spirit, I really want to be a blessing, and I know I have buttons, and I know You know where they are. Please help me find one small button." He immediately put a picture in my mind, then I walked straight over to a hidden drawer I had completely forgotten about and opened it, and right in front of my eyes was one small button. In the moment I was so grateful and blown away by His generosity and willingness to help with something so seemingly unimportant.

The next day, I woke up grieving about my faux pas—the fact that I had turned my whole house upside down before I asked the Lord for help.

*I was recently talking with a friend about how there is no female pastor on staff at my church to attempt to connect with. Today, the Lord pieced the two situations together and brought revelation.*

*I haven't taken some things to Him yet because they don't seem important enough. Subconsciously, I wanted a leadership connection to which I could take "everything."*

*God forgive me! I know You'll provide that connection somehow, as You always have because it's biblical. You specifically designed me to understand its necessity and value, but, Lord, don't let me replace You with anyone. Lord, thank You for fresh insight into how intricately and intimately involved in my life You desire to be! According to Your Word, You know how many hairs are on my head... That's a lot of keeping track, Lord. You said Your thoughts about me outnumber the grains of sand on the seashore.*

*Lord help me! I want to grow in my intimacy with You to the degree You are first and foremost in every thought in my life—grand and infinitesimal, important, and those deemed unimportant... Put the inclination in my heart to want to seek You first (and remind me to seek You first!) and to honor Your omnipresence with even the most minute details of my life. In Jesus' name, amen!*

CHAPTER 14:

# CONVERSATIONS FROM

# THE BIBLE

These passages highlight the continuous and varied communication between God and humans in both the Old and New Testaments. They reveal His desire for relationships through His active participation in their lives. They also show His unwavering commitment to guiding and sustaining His people throughout history. From Genesis to Revelation, you can see how passionately God has pursued a relationship with us. I hope you find a new level of confidence in God's desire to have an intimate relationship with you as you read these interactions and search out and reflect on the means by which He communicated with each character.

Genesis 3:8-13 - Adam and Eve: God questions Adam and Eve after their disobedience in the Garden.

Genesis 4:9-15 - Cain: God questions Cain about his brother Abel's whereabouts following Abel's murder.

Genesis 6:13-22 - Noah: God instructs Noah to build the ark in anticipation of the flood.

Genesis 12:1-3 - Abraham: God calls Abram to leave his home and go to a land He would show him, promising blessing and a great nation.

Genesis 13:14-17 - Abraham: After Lot separates from Abram, God promises the land to Abram's descendants.

Genesis 15:1-21 - Abraham: God makes a covenant with Abram, promising him numerous descendants and the land.

Genesis 17:1-22 - Abraham: God establishes the covenant of circumcision with Abraham and renames him.

Genesis 18:1-33 - Abraham: Abraham speaks with the Lord about the fate of Sodom and Gomorrah.

Genesis 21:12-13 - Abraham: God tells Abraham to listen to Sarah regarding Hagar and Ishmael.

Genesis 22:1-18 - Abraham: God tests Abraham's faith by asking him to sacrifice Isaac.

Genesis 26:2-5 - Isaac: God instructs Isaac not to go to Egypt and reaffirms the Abrahamic covenant with him.

Genesis 28:12-15 - Jacob: Jacob dreams of a ladder reaching to heaven and speaks with God, who renews the covenant made with Abraham.

Genesis 31:3 - Jacob: God tells Jacob to return to the land of his fathers.

Genesis 31:24 - Laban: God warns Laban not to harm Jacob.

Genesis 32:24-30 - Jacob: Jacob wrestles with God and is renamed Israel.

Genesis 35:1 - Jacob: God instructs Jacob to go to Bethel and make an altar.

Genesis 35:9-12 - Jacob: God appears to Jacob again and blesses him.

Genesis 46:2-4 - Jacob: God speaks to Israel in visions of the night as he moves to Egypt.

Exodus 3:1-10 - Moses: God speaks to Moses from a burning bush, calling him to lead the Israelites out of Egypt.

Exodus 4:1-17 - Moses: God gives Moses signs to prove His mission to the Israelites and Pharaoh.

Exodus 6:2-8 - Moses: God reaffirms His covenant with Moses, outlining His plan to rescue Israel.

Exodus 12:1-13 - Moses and Aaron: God gives them instructions for the Passover.

Exodus 13:17-22 - Israelites: God leads the people out of Egypt by a pillar of cloud and fire.

Exodus 14:15-16 - Moses: God instructs Moses to part the Red Sea.

Exodus 19:3-6 - Moses: God gives instructions on Sinai before dictating the Ten Commandments.

Exodus 20:1-17 - Israelites: God gives the Ten Commandments directly to the people.

Exodus 24:12-18 - Moses: God calls Moses to receive the stone tablets with the law.

Exodus 31:1-11 - Bezalel and Oholiab: God chooses and fills them with the Spirit of God to craft the Tabernacle.

Exodus 32:7-14 - Moses: God and Moses discuss the Israelites' idolatry with the golden calf.

Exodus 33:1-3 - Israelites: God tells the people He will send an angel to lead them into the Promised Land.

Exodus 33:11 - Moses: Moses speaks to God face to face as a man speaks to his friend.

Exodus 34:1-28 - Moses: Moses renews the tablets and covenant after the golden calf incident.

Exodus 40:34-38 - Israelites: God's glory fills the Tabernacle.

Leviticus 1:1-2 - Moses: God gives instructions on burnt offerings.

Numbers 7:89 - Moses: Moses hears the voice of God speaking from above the mercy seat.

Numbers 12:4-8 - Miriam and Aaron: God explains why He speaks directly and clearly to Moses, distinguishing him from other prophets.

Numbers 14:11-20 - Moses: God discusses Israel's unbelief, and Moses intercedes.

Numbers 16:20-35 - Korah, Dathan, and Abiram: God delivers His judgment on the rebels.

Numbers 22:9-35 - Balaam: God speaks to Balaam through his donkey and an angel.

Deuteronomy 1:6-8 - Moses: God reminds Israel of His command to leave Horeb and possess the land.

Deuteronomy 31:14-23 - Moses and Joshua: God commissions Joshua in the presence of Moses.

Deuteronomy 34:4 - Moses: God shows Moses the Promised Land before his death.

Joshua 1:1-9 - Joshua: God commands Joshua to lead Israel and be strong.

Joshua 5:13-15 - Joshua: The commander of the Lord's army appears to Joshua near Jericho.

Judges 6:11-24 - Gideon: The angel of the Lord calls Gideon to save Israel from Midian.

Judges 7:2-8 - Gideon: God instructs Gideon to reduce his army to 300 men.

Judges 13:3-23 - Manoah and his wife: The angel of the Lord foretells the birth of Samson.

1 Samuel 3:1-14 - Samuel: God calls young Samuel by name in the night, marking his prophetic ministry.

1 Samuel 9:15-17 - Samuel: God reveals to Samuel that Saul will be king.

1 Samuel 16:1-13 - Samuel: God directs Samuel to anoint David as king.

2 Samuel 2:1 - David: God instructs David to go to Hebron.

2 Samuel 5:17-25 - David: God gives David battle strategies against the Philistines.

2 Samuel 7:4-17 - David: God sends Nathan to tell David his son will build the temple.

2 Samuel 12:1-15 - David: Nathan delivers God's judgment to David for his sin with Bathsheba.

2 Samuel 24:10-17 - David: God gives David three options as a consequence for his sin of conducting a census.

1 Kings 3:5 15  Solomon: God appears to Solomon in a dream, offering him anything he asks.

1 Kings 6:11-13 - Solomon: God makes a promise to Solomon during the temple construction.

1 Kings 9:1-9 - Solomon: God appears to Solomon again after the temple is built.

1 Kings 11:9-13 - Solomon: God rebukes Solomon for his idolatry.

1 Kings 12:22-24 - Rehoboam: Through Shemaiah, God tells Rehoboam not to fight the northern tribes.

1 Kings 17:1-16 - Elijah: Elijah prophesies a drought and is then told by God to hide by the brook Cherith.

1 Kings 18:1 - Elijah: God tells Elijah to present himself to Ahab.

1 Kings 19:9-18 - Elijah: God speaks to Elijah in a still small voice on Mount Horeb.

1 Kings 21:17-29 - Ahab: Elijah delivers God's judgment to Ahab for his and Jezebel's actions against Naboth.

2 Kings 1:3-4 - Ahaziah: Elijah is told by God to confront Ahaziah's messengers regarding their seeking advice from Baal-Zebub.

2 Kings 1:15-16 - Elijah: God tells Elijah to go down with the captain of the king's guard after showing he is a man of God.

2 Kings 2:1 - Elijah and Elisha: God plans to take Elijah to heaven in a whirlwind.

2 Kings 3:11-20 - Elisha: God delivers a message through Elisha about how He will provide water and give Moab into Israel's hands.

2 Kings 4:1-7 - The widow: Elisha tells the widow how to miraculously multiply her oil to pay her debts and save her sons from slavery.

2 Kings 5:8-14 - Naaman: Elisha sends a message to Naaman to wash in the Jordan River to be healed of leprosy.

2 Kings 6:8-23 - Elisha: Elisha prays for his servant's eyes to be opened to see the army of the Lord.

2 Kings 7:1-2 - Elisha: Elisha prophesies an end to the famine in Samaria.

2 Kings 9:1-10 - Jehu: Elisha instructs one of the sons of the prophets to anoint Jehu as king over Israel.

2 Kings 13:14-19 - Elisha and Joash: Elisha instructs King Joash to strike the ground with arrows, symbolizing Israel's future victories.

2 Kings 19:6-7 - Hezekiah: Isaiah delivers God's message to Hezekiah concerning the Assyrian king Sennacherib.

2 Kings 19:20-34 - Hezekiah: God promises Hezekiah deliverance from the Assyrians, fulfilled when an angel strikes down 185,000 Assyrians.

2 Kings 20:1-11 - Hezekiah: God tells Hezekiah through Isaiah that he will be healed and live an additional 15 years.

2 Kings 20:16-18 - Hezekiah: Isaiah predicts the Babylonian captivity of Judah.

2 Kings 22:14-20 - Josiah: Huldah the prophetess foretells disaster because the people have forsaken God, but reassures Josiah because of his humility before God.

2 Kings 24:2-4 - Jehoiakim: God sends Babylonian, Aramean, Moabite, and Ammonite raiders against Jehoiakim because of his evil deeds.

2 Kings 25:1-21 - Zedekiah: Jerusalem is besieged and eventually destroyed as God's judgment for the sins of Manasseh and the people's refusal to listen.

1 Chronicles 11:1-3 - David: All Israel comes to David at Hebron and tells him that God said he would shepherd His people.

1 Chronicles 17:1-15 - David: God sends Nathan to tell David he is not to build the temple, but his son will.

1 Chronicles 22:6-11 - Solomon: David gives Solomon God's message about building the temple.

2 Chronicles 11:2-4 - Rehoboam: God tells Rehoboam through Shemaiah the prophet not to fight against the northern tribes of Israel.

2 Chronicles 12:5-8 - Rehoboam: Shemaiah delivers a prophecy to Rehoboam and the leaders of Judah that because they have forsaken God, He has forsaken them to Shishak.

2 Chronicles 15:1-7 - Asa: Azariah, son of Oded, prophesies to Asa, encouraging him to reform Judah.

2 Chronicles 18:18-22 - Ahab: Micaiah describes a vision of the heavenly court where a spirit volunteers to entice Ahab into battle.

2 Chronicles 20:14-17 - Jehoshaphat: Jahaziel prophesies that God will give Judah victory over their enemies.

2 Chronicles 24:19-22 - Joash: Zechariah, son of Jehoiada, prophesies against Judah for abandoning the Lord, which leads to his death.

2 Chronicles 28:9-15 - Ahaz: A prophet named Oded warns the Samaritans against enslaving their fellow Israelites from Judah.

2 Chronicles 34:22-28 - Josiah: Huldah the prophetess confirms the authenticity of the Book of the Law found in the temple and foretells the disaster described therein.

2 Chronicles 36:12-16 - Zedekiah and Judah: Jeremiah and other prophets warn Zedekiah and the people, but they do not listen.

Nehemiah 1:4-11 - Nehemiah: Nehemiah's prayer includes God's promise to gather His people if they return to Him.

Nehemiah 4:4-5 - Nehemiah: Nehemiah prays to God about the taunts of Judah's enemies and asks God to turn their insults back on their own heads.

Nehemiah 6:9 - Nehemiah: Nehemiah prays for strength to continue the work despite opposition.

Nehemiah 9:6-37 - Levites: The Levites lead the people in a prayer of confession recounting God's faithfulness and their ancestors' disobedience.

Esther 4:16 - Esther: Esther asks Mordecai to gather all the Jews in Susa to fast for her as she plans to approach the king unsummoned, implying her dependence on God's intervention.

Job 1:6-12 - Job: Satan presents himself before God, and they discuss Job's integrity.

Job 2:1-6 - Job: God and Satan have a second conversation about Job's affliction.

Job 38:1-41 - Job: God answers Job out of the whirlwind and challenges his understanding of the universe.

Job 40:1-5 - Job: Job responds to God's challenges with humility.

Job 42:1-6 - Job: Job repents in dust and ashes after God questions him.

Psalm 3:4 - David: David mentions that he cried to the Lord, and He answered him from His holy hill.

Psalm 4:1 - David: David calls out to God for relief from distress, and God enlarges him.

Psalm 18:6 - David: In distress, David calls to the Lord, Who hears from His temple.

Psalm 22:1-31 - David: David cries out to God and discusses God's deliverance.

Psalm 28:6-9 - David: David blesses God, Who has heard the voice of his supplications.

Psalm 31:22 - David: David praises God for His goodness, which he had doubted.

Psalm 34:4 - David: David seeks the Lord, and He answers him, delivering him from all his fears.

Psalm 91:15 - The faithful: God promises to answer those who call on Him, delivering and honoring them.

Psalm 120:1 - David: David calls to the Lord in his distress, and God answers him.

Psalm 138:3 - David: Upon David's prayer, God makes him bold with strength in his soul.

Proverbs 1:23 - Wisdom: Wisdom personified promises to pour out her spirit to those who listen.

Isaiah 6:8-13 - Isaiah: Isaiah hears the voice of the Lord asking, "Whom shall I send?" and he responds, leading to his commission as a prophet.

Isaiah 38:1-5 - Hezekiah: God sends Isaiah to tell King Hezekiah that his prayer has been heard and his life will be extended.

Isaiah 40:1-5 - Isaiah: God speaks comfort to Jerusalem, declaring the coming of the Lord and the preparation needed.

Isaiah 49:1-6 - Servant of the Lord: The servant hears God and is called from the womb to bring Jacob back to Him.

Jeremiah 1:4-10 - Jeremiah: God calls Jeremiah to be a prophet to the nations, equipping him with His words.

Jeremiah 7:1-7 - Jeremiah: God instructs Jeremiah to stand at the gate of the Lord's house and deliver a message of repentance.

Jeremiah 11:1-5 - Jeremiah: God reminds Jeremiah of the covenant He made with the ancestors of the Israelites when He brought them out of Egypt.

Jeremiah 13:1-11 - Jeremiah: God instructs Jeremiah to carry out a symbolic act with a linen belt to represent the close bond He desired with Israel, which they corrupted.

Jeremiah 29:10-14 - Exiles in Babylon: God promises the exiles He will bring them back after 70 years and they will find Him when they seek Him with all their heart.

Jeremiah 31:31-34 - House of Israel and Judah: God promises a new covenant, different from the one made when He took their ancestors out of Egypt.

Ezekiel 1:1-28 - Ezekiel: In visions of God, Ezekiel sees the likeness of four living creatures and hears the voice of God from above the expanse.

Ezekiel 2:1-3:27 - Ezekiel: God calls Ezekiel to speak to the Israelites, giving him a scroll to eat and the words to say.

Ezekiel 18:1-32 - Israelites: God explains His way of individual responsibility for sin and righteousness.

Ezekiel 33:1-33 - Ezekiel: God appoints Ezekiel as a watchman for Israel to warn them of coming danger.

Daniel 2:19-23 - Daniel: In a night vision, God reveals to Daniel the mystery of King Nebuchadnezzar's dream.

Daniel 9:20-23 - Daniel: While Daniel is praying for understanding, Gabriel comes to give him insight and understanding of the prophecy.

Daniel 10:10-14 - Daniel: An angel touches Daniel and explains the delay in his coming due to a spiritual battle.

Hosea 1:2-10 - Hosea: God instructs Hosea to marry a prostitute to symbolize Israel's unfaithfulness.

Joel 2:28-32 - Joel: God promises to pour out His Spirit on all people, prophesying the wonders in the heavens and on earth.

Amos 7:1-9 - Amos: God shows Amos visions of locusts, fire, and a plumb line as symbols of judgment against Israel.

Jonah 1:1-2 - Jonah: God commands Jonah to go to Nineveh and preach against its wickedness.

Micah 6:1-8 - Israel: God pleads with Israel over His requirements and recounts His righteous acts.

Zephaniah 1:1-18 - Zephaniah: God communicates through Zephaniah a sweeping message of judgment against Judah and the whole world.

Haggai 1:1-15 - Haggai: Through Haggai, God challenges the people about their priorities in rebuilding the temple.

Zechariah 1:1-17 - Zechariah: Zechariah receives visions encouraging the people to return to the Lord.

Malachi 1:1-5 - Israel: God expresses His love for Israel and contrasts it with His judgment on Edom.

Matthew 1:20-24 - Joseph: An angel appears to Joseph in a dream, reassuring him to take Mary as his wife because her child is from the Holy Spirit.

Matthew 2:12-13 - Joseph: God warns Joseph in a dream to flee to Egypt with Mary and Jesus to escape Herod's massacre.

Matthew 2:19-20 - Joseph: After Herod's death, an angel tells Joseph it is safe to return to Israel.

Matthew 3:16-17 - Jesus: At Jesus' baptism, a voice from heaven declares, "This is my beloved Son, with Whom I am well pleased."

Matthew 4:1-11 - Jesus: Jesus is led by the Spirit into the wilderness to be tempted by the devil and converses with him, countering each temptation with scripture.

Matthew 17:1-5 - Peter, James, and John: During the Transfiguration of Jesus, they hear the voice of God from the cloud saying, "This is My beloved Son, with Whom I am well pleased; listen to Him."

Mark 1:10-11 - Jesus: At His baptism, Jesus hears the voice of God affirming His sonship.

Luke 1:11-20 - Zechariah: The angel Gabriel tells Zechariah that his wife Elizabeth will bear a son named John.

Luke 1:26-38 - Mary: Gabriel appears to Mary, announcing she will conceive Jesus, the Son of the Most High.

Luke 2:8-14 - Shepherds: An angel announces Jesus' birth to the shepherds, followed by a multitude of heavenly hosts praising God.

Luke 2:25-35 - Simeon: The Holy Spirit reveals to Simeon he would not die before seeing the Christ. When Jesus is presented at the temple, Simeon prophesies about Jesus' future.

Luke 2:36-38 - Anna: Anna the prophetess gives thanks to God and speaks about the child Jesus to all who were looking for the redemption of Jerusalem.

Luke 3:21-22 - Jesus: During His baptism, the heavens open, and God's voice declares Jesus as His beloved Son.

Luke 9:28-36 - Peter, James, and John: They witness Jesus' Transfiguration and hear God's voice affirming Jesus.

John 12:28-30 - Jesus: Jesus asks for God's name to be glorified, and a voice from heaven responds, heard by the crowd as thunder.

Acts 1:4-8 - Apostles: Jesus instructs His apostles to wait in Jerusalem for the Holy Spirit.

Acts 2:1-4 - Apostles: The Holy Spirit comes upon the apostles, allowing them to speak in other tongues as the Spirit gives them utterance.

Acts 8:26-29 - Philip: An angel of the Lord tells Philip to go south to the road that goes down from Jerusalem to Gaza. The Spirit tells him to approach the Ethiopian eunuch's chariot.

Acts 9:3-6 - Saul (Paul): On the road to Damascus, Paul encounters a blinding light and hears Jesus' voice asking why he persecutes Him.

Acts 10:3-6; 10:9-16 - Cornelius and Peter: Cornelius sees an angel in a vision instructing him to send for Peter; Peter has a vision about clean and unclean animals, preparing him to accept Gentile believers.

Acts 12:7-11 - Peter: An angel frees Peter from prison, guiding him past guards.

Acts 13:2 - Barnabas and Saul (Paul): While fasting and praying, the Holy Spirit tells the Antioch church to set Barnabas and Saul apart for God's work.

Acts 16:6-10 - Paul: Paul has a vision of a man of Macedonia asking for help, directing his missionary journey.

Acts 18:9-10 - Paul: In a vision, God tells Paul not to be afraid and to keep speaking in Corinth because God has many people in the city.

Acts 22:17-21 - Paul: Paul recounts a vision where he was praying in the temple and fell into a trance, seeing Jesus telling him to leave Jerusalem quickly.

Acts 23:11 - Paul: The Lord stands by Paul and tells him he must testify in Rome as he has in Jerusalem.

Acts 27:23-24 - Paul: An angel tells Paul he must stand before Caesar and that God has granted safety to all sailing with him.

Revelation 1:1-20 - John: John receives a vision on the island of Patmos, where Jesus appears and instructs him to write to the seven churches.

Revelation 4:1 - John: A voice like a trumpet invites John to come up to heaven to see what must take place after this.

Revelation 5:1-14 - John: In a vision, John sees the heavenly worship of the Lamb who was able to open the scroll.

Revelation 7:9-17 - John: John sees a great multitude from every nation worshiping before the throne, and their praises are explained by one of the elders.

Revelation 10:8-11 - John: John is told to take a little scroll from an angel and eat it; it tastes sweet but turns bitter in his stomach.

Revelation 11:1-12 - John: John is given a measuring rod to measure the temple of God, and he sees the two witnesses prophesy and ascend to heaven.

Revelation 12:1-17 - John: John sees a vision of a woman clothed with the sun, the moon under her feet, and a crown of twelve stars on her head being persecuted by a dragon.

Revelation 14:1-20 - John: John sees the Lamb standing on Mount Zion with 144,000 who had His name and His Father's name written on their foreheads.

Revelation 19:1-16 - John: John hears the multitude in heaven praising God for the wedding supper of the Lamb and sees the Rider on the White Horse, who is called Faithful and True.

Revelation 21:1-8 - John: John sees a new heaven and a new earth and hears a loud voice from the throne saying that God's dwelling place is now among the people.

Revelation 22:12-17 - John: Jesus declares He is coming soon, and John hears the Spirit and the bride say, "Come."

# CONCLUSION:

## Invitation

Consider this an open invitation to explore a friendship with God on your own terms, especially if you are skeptical or feel disillusioned by past experiences. Start where you are and keep an open heart. You don't need to have all the answers or rigidly establish a bunch of rules to begin. Your relationship with God, like every meaningful relationship, will take time to develop and will grow deeper as you interact more with Him.

Read about Him, talk to Him and about Him, pour your heart out to Him, and ask Him questions; just remember it is equally important to listen to Him. You'll find that He speaks in ways and through means you never expected. Whether through the words of a leader or friend, the beauty of creation, the still small voice in your head, pictures in your mind, or the pages of the Bible, God has countless ways of revealing Himself to those who seek Him. This exploration only requires a simple, sincere step towards getting to know God as He truly is—a step towards the most significant relationship you'll ever have.

As you continue this relationship adventure, I pray you grow in the deep genuine intimacy with God that He seeks. He is present and active in every aspect of your life and eager for an intimate friendship with you. I pray you become more and more aware of His constant nearness and love for you.

As we draw this time to a close—a time of deepening our friendship with God—it's exciting to reflect on the ground we've covered together, from understanding the heart and nature of God and His personal invitation to you for friendship to embracing practical daily habits to help you hone in with

Him, including how to make the most of the invaluable support of your community.

Let's look at some key takeaways from our time together: We highlighted God's relentless pursuit of you and His desire for intimacy; we've learned that deepening your friendship with God isn't about doing religious duties but engaging in a constant personal, life-giving exchange with Him; and we've learned to live every moment aware that He wants to communicate with you, whether through prayer, trials, scripture reading, worship, circumstances, and so much more.

Reflecting on this transformational odyssey of reading and embracing the truths in this book, consider how your understanding of and relationship with God might have shifted. Remember, transformation is an ongoing journey of processes—a beautiful, continuous shaking off of who you are NOT, to reveal the Christ within. It's about becoming more like Christ, experiencing and then expressing His love more deeply. Each step is significant, no matter how small it may seem.

I hope you are encouraged to keep nurturing this precious relationship. Let your lifestyle be one of curiosity and growth by staying open to learning more about God, seeking Him in every area of your life, and allowing the Holy Spirit to guide, shape, and mold you day by day.

I invite you to keep the relational momentum going. Share how this book has impacted your life, connect with others who want a deeper friendship with God, and perhaps join or start a group in your church or community where you can do life together and enjoy this expedition in a fellowship setting.

Thank you for sharing this quest with me. Let's continue enjoying the incredible friendship with God that He offers to each of us.

Let's close this time together with prayer:

"Dear Heavenly Father, we come with hearts full of gratitude for the journey of processes You're walking us through. Thank You for the revelation of Your love and faithfulness. We will continue to seek a deeper friendship with You, so grant us the courage and boldness to live out the truths we've discovered. Enliven our minds with the awareness of Your presence, every moment of every day. May our lives reflect Your glory, and may our stories inspire others to seek You, too. In Jesus' name, Amen."

Hello Wonderful Reader,

I hope you've enjoyed "The Ultimate Guide to Friendship with God"! I wanted to take a moment to talk about something that can truly make a difference—not just for you but for others as well.

"To the world, you may be one person, but to one person, you may be the world." – Dr. Seuss

Your unique experience with this book is invaluable; now, you can share that value with others. Imagine the impact you could have by sharing your thoughts and experiences with this book. Your insights could be the guidance someone else needs on their own journey to deepen their relationship with God.

Your words can guide others to find the right resources for their spiritual journey, becoming a beacon and lighting the way. Your review can help others decide if "The Ultimate Guide to Friendship with God" is the right tool for them.

We kindly ask you to take a few moments to leave an honest review. It's a small action that can create a huge impact. Simply go to Amazon, search for the book title, and scroll down to leave your review. It's as easy as that!

Just think about the joy of knowing that your insights are helping others on their journey with God. You're not just leaving a review; you're sharing your wisdom and making a significant difference.

So, dear reader, let's pay it forward together and help others discover the greatness of "The Ultimate Guide to Friendship with God." Your review might be the encouragement someone else needs!

With heartfelt gratitude,

Arm In Arm Publishing Team

# Check out other amazing products for all ages at

# www.ArmInArmPublishing.com

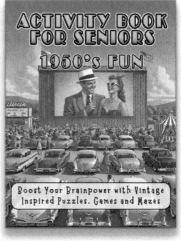

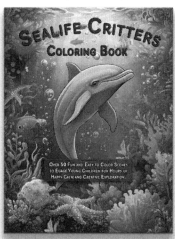

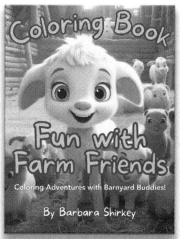

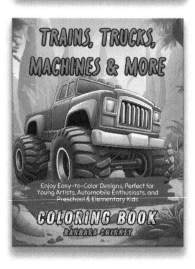

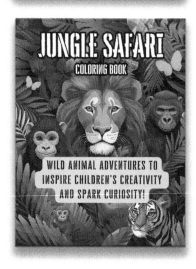

# References

*Amplified Bible, Classic Edition.* (1987). Lockman Foundation.

*Holy Bible, New International Version.* (2011). Biblica, Inc.

*Holy Bible, New Living Translation.* (2015). Tyndale House Foundation.

*New King James Version.* (1982). Thomas Nelson.

Tenney, Tommy. (1998). *The God Chasers: My Soul Follows Hard After Thee.* Destiny Image Publishers. (This book contains various illustrations and teachings on the depth of worship and pursuing God's presence.)

*The Holy Bible, English Standard Version.* (2016). Crossway.

*The Holy Bible, King James Version.* (2017). King James Bible Online. https://www.kingjamesbibleonline.org/ (Original work published 1769).

*The Passion Translation.* (2020). Passion & Fire Ministries, Inc.

Made in United States
Orlando, FL
02 December 2024

54874306R00089